D1637133

James Monroe

5th President of the United States

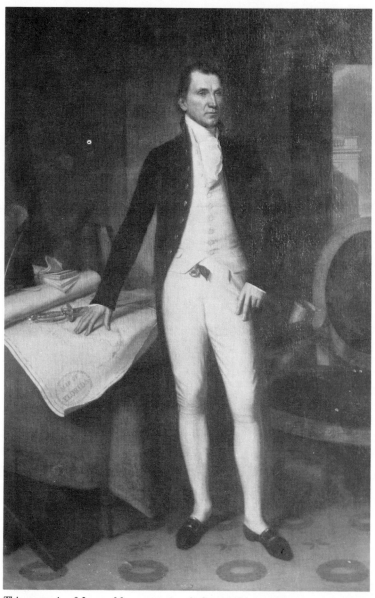

This portrait of James Monroe, painted about 1820 by John Vanderlyn, shows the President standing in the White House. (New York City Art Commission.)

James Monroe

5th President of the United States

Rebecca Stefoff

GARRETT EDUCATIONAL CORPORATION

Manufactured in the United States of America

Edited and produced by Synthegraphics Corporation

Library of Congress Cataloging in Publication Data

Stefoff, Rebecca, 1951–
  James Monroe: 5th president of the United States.

  (Presidents of the United States)
  Bibliography: p.
  Includes index.
  Summary: Profiles the early life, career, family, and contributions of the fifth president of the United States.
  1. Monroe, James, 1758–1831—Juvenile literature.
2. Presidents—United States—Biography—Juvenile literature. [1. Monroe, James, 1758–1831. 2. Presidents]
I. Title. II. Series.
E372.S74 1988   973.5′4 [B] [92]   87-32845
ISBN 0-944483-11-9

Contents

Chronology for James Monroe

1758 Born on April 28

1774–
1776 Attended College of William and Mary

1776– Served as an officer in the Continental
1781 Army

1782 Member of Virginia House of Delegates

1783– Member of the Congress of the
1786 Confederation

1786 Married Elizabeth Kortright; elected to
Virginia House of Delegates

1790– Served as U.S. senator from Virginia
1794

1794 Appointed minister to France

1799– Elected governor of Virginia three times
1802 in a row

1803 Appointed by Thomas Jefferson as
minister to France; helped make
Louisiana Purchase

1803– Served as minister to England and
1807 Spain

1811 Elected governor of Virginia for the
fourth time; appointed secretary of state
by James Madison

1814– Served as secretary of war and secretary
1815 of state

1817– Served as fifth President of the United
1825 States

1831 Died on July 4

Chapter 1

A Revolutionary Hero

Christmas Day, 1776, was cold and bleak in Pennsylvania. Wet, heavy snow fell all day and into the night. The Delaware River, dividing Pennsylvania and New Jersey, was whipped by a freezing wind and clogged with floating cakes of ice. And on this unlikely evening, the wintry valley between these two states was the scene of one of the most famous river voyages of all time: General George Washington's crossing of the Delaware. It became one of the best-known events of the American Revolution.

Washington crossed from Pennsylvania into New Jersey to attack a garrison of about 1,400 Hessian soldiers at Trenton. The Hessians, from the German duchy of Hesse, were mercenaries in the service of the British. They were well-armed, experienced fighters. The Americans were a less-polished fighting force; most were inexperienced in battle. Many of them were farmers armed with their hunting guns. Some of them—like 18-year-old Lieutenant James Monroe— were young. Their greatest weapon was their determination: they were fighting for their freedom from British domination and they refused to give up. The United States had declared its independence from England just months before. Americans knew that during the coming months the issue of independence would be decided on the battlefield.

Crossing the Delaware required all the courage and determination the Americans possessed. Washington divided his troops into three groups. He took command of the group that included the Third Virginia Infantry, to which Lieutenant Monroe belonged. Command of the other two groups was given to two high-ranking officers. Washington's plan was to cross the river as soon as darkness fell and then to march rapidly on Trenton.

It was six o'clock in the evening when Washington and his group clambered into boats at the small riverside village of McKonkey's Ferry (now called Washington Crossing). Each man carried three days' worth of food and 40 rounds of ammunition—a pathetically small amount of ammunition with which to confront the larger force of better-equipped Hessians. The two other groups of Americans were to cross the Delaware at other points, but they could not do so because of the terrible condition of the ice-clogged river.

However, Washington and his men made it across. The harsh wind stung their faces with driving snow and tugged at their cloaks. Swirling snow and pitch darkness made it impossible to see the opposite shore. The boats collided again and again with massive chunks of floating ice. Miraculously, they fought their way to the opposite bank.

AN IMPORTANT MISSION

Monroe was one of 50 soldiers from Virginia who had volunteered to land first. His commanding officer, Captain William Washington, had an important mission. He was supposed to hurry with his men to the main northbound road, about a mile and a half away, and close the road so that the enemy garrison at Trenton could not send to Princeton for reinforcements. Monroe was posted, with a handful of men and a field gun, at the intersection of the Pennington and the Lawrenceville roads. His orders were to let no one pass.

Monroe carried out his orders well. He and his men arrived at their post without being seen by enemy sentries. However, soon after taking his position Monroe was challenged. A nearby farmer had heard his dogs barking and went out into the stormy night to see what was causing the disturbance. Approaching the crossroads, he angrily ordered the soldiers off his land.

"I am sorry to trouble you, sir, but we will not leave," Monroe replied politely.

"Darn you, I said to get out of here at once! Do you want me to set my dogs on you?" cried the farmer in a rage. He began to shout and swear. Monroe caught the words "miserable Hessians."

"Sir, we are American soldiers in the service of General Washington," he said firmly. "Now, either you'll go home quietly or we'll be forced to arrest you."

The farmer stared open-mouthed at the stern young officer, then let out a roar of laughter. "Americans, is it?" he said. "Why, lads, I thought you were more of those cursed Hessians!"

The now-friendly farmer urged Monroe and his men to come in out of the storm and warm themselves by his fire. But, although some of his men stared longingly at the snug farmhouse, Monroe said, "Thank you kindly, but our orders are not to move from this spot."

"Well, orders must be obeyed," replied the farmer with a smile. He went home — and returned not an hour later with hot drinks and food for the shivering men. He informed Monroe that he was a doctor, then he spent the rest of the night at the crossroads with Monroe, refusing to go home. The young lieutenant felt encouraged that the local citizens detested the Hessians and were eager to side with the revolutionary army.

General Washington had wanted his attack on the Hessians to take place at dawn. But by the time his men and artillery had been ferried across the river and marched to the outskirts of Trenton, he was falling behind schedule. Washington and his troops arrived at the Pennington–Lawrenceville crossroads just before dawn. Lieutenant Monroe, his heart pounding with excitement, swung into place in the marching column.

THE BATTLE AFTER THE CROSSING

Washington directed the Battle of Trenton from atop a nearby hill. Captains Thomas Forrest and Alexander Hamilton were assigned to fire batteries of cannon down several of the main streets of the town. A unit under Captain William Washington and Lieutenant Monroe was held in reserve at the end of King Street, which led to the Hessian barracks.

At a given signal, the American guns began firing. Soon the sleepy town was in an uproar. Drums rallied the startled Hessian troops, men shouted as they hurried to their battle stations, muskets barked, and through it all the cannon boomed. About a quarter of a mile from their barracks, a line of Hessian soldiers blocked King Street, firing their own cannon back up the street at the advancing Americans. Captain Washington and Lieutenant Monroe were ordered to break the Hessian defense.

They didn't hesitate. Waving their double-edged bayonets, they led their Virginians in a frenzied charge, causing the Hessians to fall back. Their attack was so sudden and fierce, it is said, that 20 British soldiers who shared the barracks with the Hessians took to their horses and galloped away.

The beleaguered Hessians moved up two brass three-pounders (cannon that fired three-pound shells) in an attempt to hold back the Americans. Hacking away with their bayonets, Washington and Monroe dashed forward to capture the guns. The Hessians retreated, and the way was clear for the Americans to advance down King Street to the barracks. General Washington had left the hilltop and was now riding down the street, just behind the vanguard of Virginians.

Taking Command

Suddenly, volleys of musket fire exploded from the barracks as the Hessians trapped inside made a last stand. Over the din of the battle, Monroe heard a cry and saw his leader, Captain Washington, fall wounded to the ground. A second's hesitation, Monroe knew, could cause the Americans to lose momentum. They might even panic under the hail of Hessian fire and throw victory away.

That must not happen! Monroe leaped ahead in Washington's place, waving his sword overhead to guide the men behind him. Shouting encouragement, he led the American troops at a run toward the last line of the Hessian defense. General Washington, who was only yards away, spoke later of Monroe's bravery, marveling at his disregard of danger.

Monroe's wild charge carried him right up to the enemy line. Suddenly, a musket ball ripped through his left shoulder and into his upper arm. Dazed with pain and shock and bleeding heavily, Monroe lost consciousness. His last thought was that victory was assured for the Americans.

The young lieutenant was lucky. He was carried back to the quiet end of King Street. There the farmer-doctor who had befriended Monroe and his men at the crossroads the night before was tending the American wounded. He saw that the bullet had severed one of Monroe's arteries. Quickly, he tied off the artery before more blood could be lost, and saved Monroe's life.

Recuperation and Recognition

Monroe woke a few hours later back in Pennsylvania, lying in the farmhouse of William Neely in the village of Coryell's

Landing (now known as New Hope). His first question was about his superior officer. He was relieved to learn that Captain Washington was alive, although he had been shot in both hands. Next he asked about the battle, and tears of joy filled his eyes when he was told of the American victory. The Hessians had surrendered. The Americans had captured more than 1,000 prisoners, along with their stores of arms and ammunition. The Battle of Trenton was the Americans' first major victory in the War of Independence.

By the next day, Monroe had recovered enough to dictate a report of his group's activities during the battle. In a clear, straightforward way, he told of the vigil at the crossroads, the capture of the enemy three-pounders, and the charge down King Street. When General Washington read the report, he was surprised and amused to see that Monroe had given an account of the entire battle without mentioning his own heroic deeds. Washington admired Monroe's modesty; he felt that the lieutenant's heroism should be recognized. Washington immediately promoted Monroe to the rank of captain, in honor of his bravery under fire. And in his report to the Continental Congress, Washington wrote:

> Our forces were inspired by the exemplary, extraordinary conduct of Lieutenant James Monroe, Third Virginia Infantry. Second in command of the vanguard, he assumed command when Captain William Washington was wounded. His own safety meaning nothing to him, Lieutenant Monroe demonstrated courage far beyond the call of duty.
>
> I recommend that Congress offer him congratulations and enter this commendation on his personal record. I have myself, today, promoted him to the rank of Captain. Would that we had one thousand officers like him.

Monroe stayed at Neely's farm for a month; he was then moved to the house of Judge Henry Wynkoop for the final stages of recovery from his serious injury. At Judge Wynkoop's house, Monroe not only regained his health but also fell in love with the judge's daughter, Christine. Although she was already engaged to another man, Christine must have found it rather romantic to help care for this tall, handsome young war hero who had been sheltered in her father's home. After two months of recuperation, however, Captain Monroe was declared fit to return to active duty.

It was a breezy day in the early spring of 1777 when Monroe reported to the army's winter headquarters in Morristown, New Jersey, eager to return to active service. On that day, he could not have foreseen that his duty would soon take him to the western frontier, then on to France, and finally to the White House. And 40 years after being wounded at the Battle of Trenton, he would be elected the fifth President of the United States.

ALWAYS A VIRGINIAN

Monroe was born on April 28, 1758, on his father's farm in Westmoreland County, Virginia. Like most colonists in America at the time, Monroe was of British descent. His father, Spence Monroe, was from Scottish people; his mother, Elizabeth Jones Monroe, was descended from a family in Wales.

James Monroe's first ancestor in the New World arrived in 1647. He was a Scotsman, Andrew Monroe, who had commanded one of Lord Baltimore's ships. Andrew Monroe settled in Maryland. Later, after a religious quarrel with Lord Baltimore, who was the head of the Maryland settlement, Andrew moved across the Chesapeake Bay into the area known as the Northern Neck of Virginia. The Virginia government gave him a grant of land in Westmoreland County. There, on Monroe's Creek, a small stream that flowed into the

This engraving of Monroe's birthplace in Westmoreland County, Virginia, was made in about 1850. The small, plain homestead was settled in the mid-1600s by Andrew Monroe from Scotland. (Ash Lawn-Highland.)

Potomac River, he built the Monroe family home. And there, too, several generations later, James Monroe was born.

Spence Monroe, James' father, was a gentleman farmer who owned many acres of tobacco-growing land worked by slaves. Like other Monroes before him, Spence Monroe served as an officer in the local militia and as a circuit judge. The Monroes were people of substance who lived in one of the most refined areas of the American colonies. Like George Washington and Thomas Jefferson, James Monroe was raised in the tradition of well-bred Virginia families: to be courteous and honorable, to value his good name, and to know his duty to the community and his place in it. These values never left him. He always considered himself a Virginian as well as an American.

Major Boyhood Events

In later life, James Monroe seldom spoke of or wrote about his early years. As a result, little is known about his boyhood. But two events that occurred when he was young may have helped shape his political beliefs. One took place in 1765, when he was seven years old. It was the Stamp Act, passed by the English Parliament to raise taxes in the American colonies and considered unfair by many Americans. Spence Monroe and other Westmoreland County men protested against the act. It is likely that his seven-year-old son began then to be aware of the growing friction between the colonies and England.

The second event that may have contributed to Monroe's development was a visit in about 1770 from a friend of his father, Colonel George Washington, who lived in Fairfax County, Virginia. After working as a surveyor on the frontier and fighting in the French and Indian Wars, Washington had more than enough tales of travel and adventure to thrill a 12-year-old boy. In later years, much of Monroe's political

The Stamp Act

The Stamp Act that Monroe heard his elders discussing was one of the direct causes of the Revolutionary War that led to the independence of the United States. This was not the result England had in mind when the British Parliament passed the act in 1765. Its purpose was to raise money from the American colonists for use in England.

The Stamp Act did not involve postage stamps. Instead, under the act, colonists were required to pay a duty, or tax, on every piece of paper, parchment, or even animal skin used as an official document: an academic degree, a land title, a liquor license, a loan, or a lease. These items were not legal unless they had been stamped with the seal of the tax collector—thus the name Stamp Act. Newspapers, pamphlets, and almanacs were also taxed at the time of purchase, and advertisers had to pay a special tax to put their advertisements in newspapers or on posters.

The Stamp Act backfired, however. The colonists deeply and immediately resented it. Resistance to the act was so strong throughout the colonies that the British had to spend more on soldiers and officials to enforce the collection of the tax than they earned from it. Not only that, but the hated Stamp Act fueled the colonists' desire for fair representation in the British government—or, failing that, for independence.

career was concerned with freeing the American West from European claims and protecting its rights. His belief in the importance of the West may have begun as he listened to Washington's frontier stories.

Scholarly Pursuits

James Monroe went to grammar school at a small academy for boys taught by Parson Archibald Campbell. The parson's school had become a tradition for young Virginia gentlemen. He had also taught George Washington and John Marshall, who later served for 34 years as Chief Justice of the Supreme Court. Under Campbell's tutelage, Monroe mastered Latin and mathematics.

The Monroe family suffered a blow in 1774 when Spence Monroe died. At 16, James suddenly was the man of the family. (He had two younger brothers, Andrew and Joseph, and a sister, Elizabeth. Another brother had died in childhood.) James' uncle, Joseph Jones, suggested that the young man should continue his education at the College of William and Mary in Williamsburg, Virginia. James was delighted. He loved and admired his uncle, a well-known lawyer, and thought that he might also like to become a lawyer. College was the next logical step toward a law career.

At William and Mary in 1774, Monroe enrolled in the college's most difficult and challenging program. It was called the Philosophical Division, and it required the student to study Latin, Greek, English, advanced mathematics, astronomy, natural philosophy (as biology was then called), and literature. Monroe also studied chemistry and physics, read many books, and wrote essays to master logic and the art of writing. Little is known of his student career—except that he did sign a petition complaining about the dormitory food. (In spite of this small episode, the college now regards Monroe as one of its most distinguished former students.)

A Violent Turn of Events

Monroe had been at college for less than a year when, in April of 1775, alarming events began to propel the colonies toward independence. While many colonists believed that they could resist unfair British laws and still remain British colonies, others—such as the firebrand Patrick Henry—began to speak openly of fighting for freedom. Delegates elected by all the colonies except Georgia had formed the Continental Congress in Philadelphia in 1774. Change was in the air. Then, on April 19, 1775, shots were fired at Lexington and Concord in Massachusetts. And the colonies were plunged into war with England.

The very next day, before news of the events at Lexington and Concord had reached Virginia, the British schooner *Magdalen* landed at Williamsburg and took away the town's stock of gunpowder. It was clear that the British expected violence and wanted to deprive the colonists of a chance to fight. The Virginians' reaction was to form bands of militia (informal, self-trained troops). The students at the College of William and Mary formed several such bands, drilling on a green in the center of town and wearing badges with the motto "Liberty or Death." Monroe joined one of these militia companies.

For nearly a year, Monroe divided his time between drilling with the militia and studying. Like most young men in the colonies, he found it hard to keep his mind on his classes and his future career while great events were happening all around him. He learned with pride that his family's friend, George Washington, now a general, had been named commander-in-chief of the Continental Army by the Continental Congress. At this point, Monroe began to consider the possibility that his own duty lay on the battlefield rather than in the classroom.

FROM STUDENT TO SOLDIER

Monroe turned 18 in the spring of 1776. Soon afterward, he heard that Colonel Hugh Mercer, the uncle of his college friend Johnny Mercer, was forming a new regiment, the Third Virginia Infantry. Monroe's mind was made up; what was the use of studying when the struggling colonies needed every soldier they could enlist? He signed up in the Third Virginia Infantry at once.

Monroe's first opportunity to prove his valor came quickly. That June, the British governor of Virginia, Lord Dunmore, fled Williamsburg for the safety of a British man-of-war. Monroe was one of a party of soldiers that raided Dunmore's home and "liberated" his stockpile of guns and ammunition. He was promoted to lieutenant.

In July, the Continental Congress proclaimed the Declaration of Independence. There could be no turning back now—the new United States was committed to winning its complete independence from England. Monroe longed to be part of that fight. In September, he received his orders to go to the front. With other members of the Third Virginia Infantry, he was to join General Washington in New York.

Washington's Retreat

Washington had been having a poor time of it. The British Redcoats had driven his forces out of what is now Brooklyn Heights, across the East River to Manhattan Island. On the very day of Monroe's arrival at the front, the British crossed the East River in pursuit. They landed at a place called Kip's Landing, now 34th Street. The Virginians, who had just arrived on the scene, skirmished with the British in the area that is now Central Park. They held off the British advance long enough so that the rest of the Continental forces could retreat to Harlem.

More Redcoats arrived during the next month. Washington retreated north, to Westchester County. There, on October 25, the British and American armies met in the Battle of White Plains. Monroe took part in the fighting, which was so fierce that the British were forced to retreat.

But their retreat was only temporary. They mustered reinforcements and slowly pressed forward against the Americans, who fell back inch by inch. All through that dismal November, Washington's increasingly ragged forces retreated slowly across the Hudson River, through the marshy plains of northern New Jersey, to the cities of Newark, New Brunswick, Princeton, and finally Trenton.

Then, on December 7, Washington and his army crossed the Delaware from New Jersey into Pennsylvania. The British, under General William Howe, went into winter quarters at various posts throughout New Jersey. The Americans went into their winter quarters on the Pennsylvania side of the river. As winter deepened, General Washington thought constantly about the precarious situation of the Continental Army.

The Americans had been fighting the British for more than a year and a half. In the past few months, they had suffered a series of stinging defeats at the hands of the British Redcoats. Now General Washington knew he must strike a swift, sure blow to turn the tide of the war and to restore his troops' morale. He decided to leave the army's winter quarters in Pennsylvania to attack Trenton. It was a bold move, because no one expected a major attack in the dead of winter. It was also a risky one, because the river crossing was dangerous. So were the Hessian troops in Trenton. But the result of Washington's daring strategy was America's first real triumph against the British, the Battle of Trenton. Another result was that a brave young lieutenant, James Monroe of Virginia, became a war hero and a captain, ready to command a company of his own.

Chapter 2

Young Soldier and Statesman

After Monroe had fully recovered from his wound and reported to the army headquarters in the spring of 1777, he received some bad news: the Continental Army was having trouble getting men to enlist. In spite of the triumph at the Battle of Trenton and some other victories, the war was not going well for the Americans in 1777. Throughout the young and uncertain former colonies, many people were not convinced that independence would become a reality; they hesitated to commit themselves to the cause. Others were afraid to leave their homes and property, fearing that they would be looted by the British. As a result, the Continental Army simply did not have enough soldiers to serve under all the officers. Captain Monroe was one of the newly promoted commanding officers who had rank but no soldiers.

Disappointed that he didn't have any troops to command, Monroe thought that he could raise a company of soldiers in his native Virginia. He received permission to return home for an enlistment drive, but he was unable to gather enough volunteers even from among his neighbors and friends. In July, he returned to army headquarters, resolved to take whatever post he could obtain.

Carved in about 1900 by sculptor Attillio Piccirilli, this statue shows a James Monroe who probably looks much like the young Monroe of the Revolutionary years. (Ash Lawn-Highland.)

UP THROUGH THE RANKS

Monroe was offered the position of aide, or assistant, to General William Alexander, Lord Stirling. Although he held a British title, Lord Stirling lived in New Jersey and was ardently loyal to the cause of American independence. The Third Virginia Infantry was part of Stirling's brigade, so Monroe knew him and had fought under him from the time of his enlistment. As Stirling's aide, Monroe would travel with the general's troops, take part in their military actions, and also participate in officers' staff meetings and other high-level activities. Such positions had high status within the army, with relatively light responsibilities. Many other young officers envied Captain Monroe's good fortune.

On September 11, Stirling's brigade fought in the Battle of Brandywine, in eastern Pennsylvania. British Redcoats struck at the Third Virginia Infantry on the banks of Brandywine Creek and battered the American troops all day long. Nearly half the officers and a third of the enlisted men were killed or wounded. Finally, the surviving Virginians were forced to retreat to a nearby hilltop, where they were saved by the arrival of fresh troops under Washington, General Nathaniel Green, and the Marquis de Lafayette. The Marquis was wounded, and Monroe, who had escaped injury, helped him get out of the line of fire and under cover.

Monroe continued as Stirling's aide. He spent the winter of 1777–1778 with the Continental Army at Valley Forge. In the spring, he fought under Stirling at the Battle of Germantown (now part of Philadelphia), after which he was promoted to the rank of major. He also fought at the Battle of Monmouth, and he led a successful scouting expedition that gathered valuable information about the British troops and captured three prisoners.

In the summer of 1778, Monroe was promoted again,

A Bitter Winter at Valley Forge

After the battles of New York and New Jersey, the Continental Army under General George Washington spent the winter of 1777–1778 camped at Valley Forge, an area about 20 miles northwest of Philadelphia. One of the 11,000 soldiers who endured months of suffering during that historic winter was General Lord Stirling's aide, Captain James Monroe.

The disheartened troops lived in log huts. They had almost no food, clothing, or firewood, and their patrols were forced to struggle through knee-deep snow. Men wrapped their feet and legs in rags, hoping to escape frostbite. Two days before Christmas, Washington wrote: "We have this day no less than 2,873 men in camp unfit for duty because they are barefoot or otherwise naked. . . . Numbers are still obliged to sit all night by fires." But in spite of a few desertions and even rumors of mutiny, most of the soldiers tried to make the best of their grim situation. They knew that only by staying together to carry on the fight against the British in the spring could they hope to win American independence.

In February, Baron Frederick von Steuben reorganized the army. He turned the winter quarters into a training camp and drilled the troops in the military tactics that were used in his native Germany. The soldiers' morale improved with their fighting skills. In June, the once-ragged army marched out of Valley Forge as a disciplined fighting machine.

Today, Valley Forge is a national shrine. More than 2,000 acres of the Continental Army's original camp are preserved by the state of Pennsylvania as Valley Forge Park. Many of the camp buildings, including Washington's headquarters and the iron factory that gave the valley its name, have been restored. Granite markers show where regiments from each of the original 13 colonies camped. Every year, thousands of tourists from all over the United States and abroad visit the place where James Monroe and other Revolutionary patriots spent a bitter winter more than two centuries ago.

to the rank of lieutenant colonel. But although he was rising rapidly through army ranks and found many opportunities to distinguish himself as Stirling's aide, he began to grow restless. He admired and liked Stirling, yet his Virginian sense of honor felt unsatisfied. He chafed at being another man's assistant when the highest officer in the land, General Washington, had proclaimed him qualified to lead a command of his own.

Return to Virginia

Washington was sympathetic to Monroe's plight. But the problem remained: the army still did not have enough men to give Monroe a command. Once again, in the spring of 1779, Monroe returned to Virginia, hoping to raise troops. General Washington suggested to Virginia's military commander that Monroe should be given a command in the state militia. In his letter to the commander, Washington said that Monroe "had in every instance maintained the reputation of a brave, active, and sensible officer." Monroe also carried a letter of recommendation from Stirling. These testimonials could have secured him the rank of lieutenant colonel in the militia, but the state could not raise the troops to serve under him. The 21-year-old Monroe continued to be an officer without men.

Monroe then carried his letters of recommendation to Williamsburg, where the state assembly was meeting. With the letters and the help of his uncle, Jospeh Jones (now a judge), he was able to meet some of the important men in the state, including Thomas Jefferson, Virginia's first governor. Under the influence of the lively political climate in Williamsburg, Monroe began to think about a diplomatic or political career. When he heard from General Washington that there was still no prospect of getting a command, he decided to begin the law studies that had been postponed by the outbreak of war.

MONROE MEETS HIS MENTOR

Through the influence of Judge Jones, Monroe was appointed as an aide, or clerk, to Governor Jefferson. His old school friend, Johnny Mercer, also worked for the governor. The two men were responsible for helping Jefferson with his correspondence, meeting with his supporters and opponents to discuss legislation, drawing up plans and budgets, and answering the complaints of taxpayers.

In addition, Monroe and Mercer studied law under Jefferson. At that time, lawyers did not attend special law schools to obtain their legal knowledge; instead, they were apprenticed to practicing lawyers for on-the-job training. Jefferson was a respected lawyer as well as a politician, writer, philosopher, and inventor. Working closely with Jefferson,

Monroe received not only legal training but also exposure to political administration and social issues.

Monroe found that working for Jefferson suited him very well. He enjoyed political life and the intellectual discipline of the law. Most of all, he developed a deep admiration for and attachment to Jefferson. Monroe regarded Jefferson as one of the great men of his generation and felt privileged to be associated with him. But Jefferson was more than merely an employer. For Monroe, Jefferson's role was that of a mentor — a counselor, teacher, and guide who helps shape a younger person's thinking. The close and friendly relationship between the two men was to last until the end of Jefferson's life. Many of Monroe's beliefs and ideals were inherited from Jefferson, and the younger man often turned to his mentor for advice later, during his own political career.

In 1780, the capital of Virginia was moved from Williamsburg to Richmond. Now, abandoning any thought of completing his formal studies at William and Mary, Monroe followed Jefferson to the new capital and continued to serve as his aide. He was still an officer in the Continental Army, however, and in June of that year he was given a military mission.

A Command at Last

Charleston, South Carolina, had fallen to the British in May of 1780. Monroe was asked to go south to report on the situation around Charleston and to fill the post of Virginia's military commissioner to the American army in the south. He was to report to Jefferson on the movements of both American and British troops. This job was important — Jefferson and other Virginians feared that the British were planning a major attack against Virginia.

Just such an attack was indeed launched in the late summer of 1780, after Monroe had spent several months in the

Carolinas. Three thousand British troops landed at Ports-mouth. Jefferson called for men to join the militia. At last, his call was answered. More willing to defend their home state than they had been to fight under Washington in the north, Virginians now enlisted by the score. Monroe returned from his southern mission in time to take command of a regiment of recruits from Prince George County. As part of General Thomas Nelson's 800-man force, Monroe and his regiment operated in the James River area.

The war lasted for another year. During that time, Monroe served in the Virginia militia, both as a commanding officer and as a staff officer under General Muhlenberg. He was promoted to full colonel just before General Charles Cornwallis surrendered to the American forces at Yorktown, Virginia, on October 19, 1781. The great War of Independence was over.

As word of the American victory spread, joyful celebrations took place in every state and every town. A lavish Peace Ball was held at Weedon's Tavern in Fredericksburg. General Washington, General Baron von Steuben, and General "Mad" Anthony Wayne were among the guests. So was Colonel James Monroe, now 23 years old. He had played a brave and distinguished part in the birth of the new United States. Now, as he toasted the great victory, he began to wonder about his own future. He had no way of knowing that a new phase of public service was about to begin.

A POLITICAL CAREER BEGINS

Before the end of 1781, Monroe completed his law studies and passed the Virginia bar examination. He was now a lawyer, ready to practice. He sold his share of the family estate in Westmoreland and moved to Richmond. But he still was unsure what he wanted to do with himself.

Monroe dreamed of opening a law office in Richmond, saving some money, then buying land on the frontier, perhaps in the Kentucky territory. The remote, mysterious, wide-open West still stirred his imagination, as it had during his boyhood. But another dream was attractive, too—visiting Europe. He wanted to see France, but he also thought that it might be good for him to spend time in England, studying law at the Temple, the center of the legal profession in London. The dream of Europe gained strength when he learned that his friend, Colonel Josiah Parker, owned a ship that was preparing to sail for France.

Election to Virginia's House

Monroe asked for Jefferson's advice, but before the governor could respond, Monroe's choice was made for him. A group of citizens asked him to run for the House of Delegates, Virginia's state legislature. Monroe was flattered, and he began to concentrate on a political career in Virginia. Parker's ship sailed without him. Monroe would eventually spend other years in France and England, but first he would make a name for himself at home.

He was elected without opposition to the House of Delegates in April of 1782, just after his birthday. Soon after he took his seat in the assembly, a vacancy appeared on the Executive Council. This council was a committee of eight assemblymen who helped the governor administer the state's laws and business. Because Monroe had been Jefferson's aide for several years, his fellow assemblymen considered him well-qualified for the post and voted him into the council.

After his election to the council, Monroe wrote to Washington, Lord Stirling, and Jefferson to thank them for the help and support that had given him such a good start in public life. Their confidence in him was soon rewarded, for Monroe earned a reputation as a hard-working, excep-

This painting shows George Washington resigning as commander-in-chief of the Continental Army. The ceremony took place on December 23, 1783, during a meeting of the Congress of the Confederation in Annapolis, Maryland. James Monroe is seated in front of Washington, fifth from the right. James Madison is the first person on the right standing behind Monroe. (Library of Congress.)

tionally able administrator and council member. He did find time for some pleasures, however; he went to horse races, plays, and card games with John Marshall. Like Monroe, Marshall was a former pupil of Archibald Campbell and a member of the Executive Council.

Election to the Congress of the Confederation

Monroe's ability and dedication soon went beyond the limits of local politics. As a member of the House of Delegates, he quickly won the trust and respect of his fellow legislators. Then, in June of 1783, they elected him to represent Virginia in the Congress of the Confederation, the first meeting of the national government after the war, which would be held in November in Annapolis, Maryland. Monroe prepared for his new duties by visiting James Madison, who had previously held a seat in the Continental Congress, and questioning him about procedures and policies. He also spent many hours reading the long, word-for-word accounts of speeches and debates from the previous meetings of the Continental Congress.

Another member of the Virginia delegation to the Congress of the Confederation was Thomas Jefferson. He had resigned as governor, claiming to be worn out with public service. Yet he could not refuse the appeal of his fellow Virginians that he represent them in Congress. He and Monroe shared quarters in Annapolis and hired a French cook named Partout. Perhaps Monroe was still thinking of traveling to France, because he practiced his French on Partout at every opportunity.

One of the first items of business when the Congress convened in November of 1783 was a ceremony at which General Washington resigned his commission as commander-in-chief of the Continental Army. Rembrandt Peale, an American artist of the period who became famous for his many portraits of Washington, painted this scene. His painting shows Monroe sitting in front of James Madison at the ceremony. The second major event of the Congress was the ratification (passing into law) of the Treaty of Paris, which formally ended the War of Independence. Like most of the other delegates, Monroe voted in favor of this ratification in January of 1784.

Taking Sides

Up until this point, Monroe's brief experience with politics had been at the state level. Now, for the first time, he was exposed to the single most important political issue of the country's early years: the conflict between a state-oriented outlook and a national, or federal one. Businessmen, merchants, and landowners of the various regions all wanted their own interests to be protected, and many of their legislators felt that the rights or privileges of individual states must be carefully guarded. Some leaders, on the other hand, felt that the national government should be stronger than the state governments. The eventual result of this thorny issue, although not foreseen by the creators of the United States government, was the formation of political parties for the first time in the new country.

At this point in his political career, Monroe put himself on the side of those who favored national over regional or state interest. His chief reason for doing so was his strong concern for the frontier territories. These territories came under close scrutiny in Congress in 1784.

THE WESTERN FRONTIER

Most of the original 13 colonies had claimed huge territories on their western borders. In some cases, the boundaries of these territories were not very well defined. Their geography, natural resources, and Indian inhabitants remained mostly un-known. Under the Treaty of Paris, England gave up its claim to much of this land, but the frontier's status was still uncertain.

The frontiersmen who lived, farmed, and hunted in the vast Northwest Territory, which stretched beyond the tame fields of New York, Pennsylvania, and Virginia to the Mississippi River, were a hardy, independent lot. They viewed themselves and their way of life as quite different from the people and lifestyle of the settled eastern seaboard. Most fron-tiersmen wanted the territories to become independent new states. Jefferson supported their position, and so did Monroe. On the other side, Washington, Patrick Henry, and Madison were among those who felt that the existing states should enlarge themselves by extending their borders to include the frontier territories.

Just as this issue began to be hotly debated in Congress, another element entered the picture. Many regular soldiers of the Continental Army and volunteers of the various state militias had not been paid during much of the War of Inde-pendence. This was because the struggling new nation lacked either a tax-gathering mechanism or existing funds to pay them. Now that the war was over, some of these soldiers demanded payment in the form of land grants on the fron-tier. Jefferson drew up a plan dividing the frontier territories into 10 new states, and Monroe gave the plan his approval.

A Trip to the Frontier

When Congress recessed for the summer of 1784, the issue of the frontier lands was still undecided. Monroe felt that not enough members of Congress could make informed decisions about the frontier. He decided to see for himself what the Northwest Territory was like. It is possible, however, that he had more than one motive in planning a trip west—not only would he be bringing back valuable information to help him perform his congressional duties, but he would be acting out a lifelong dream of adventure on the frontier.

Monroe went first to New York City, then traveled up the Hudson River and across New York state to Niagara Falls and Lake Erie. He planned to cross what is now Ohio and return to Virginia along the Ohio River. But his plans were changed by a sudden tragedy that brought home the untamed nature of life on the frontier.

Monroe had been traveling with five other men. Upon reaching Niagara Falls, he separated from the group. The others went ahead by boat, while Monroe camped for a few days. He meant to join the group again on Lake Erie. Then word came that three of his five companions had been killed by Indians after landing on the lakeshore. Monroe was warned that it would be dangerous for him to proceed westward, especially alone. Therefore, he went to Montreal and returned to New York by way of Lake Champlain and the Hudson River.

A Design for Westward Expansion

Even though it had been cut short, his trip west had opened Monroe's eyes to the immensity and richness of the American continent. He was convinced, more than ever, that the frontier lands to the west were essential to the growth of the United States, and he was determined to support the rights and freedoms of the frontiersmen. He also had several practical suggestions for Jefferson's plan: drawing boundaries along natural borders, such as rivers and mountains, rather than along geometric lines; and also dividing the Northwest Territory into five large states, rather than 10 small ones. (Eventually, when the Northwest Territory was turned into states in the early 1800s, these suggestions were followed.)

Congress met in November in Trenton, where Monroe

had won glory in battle eight years earlier. Now he began a new battle, one to expand the United States westward and encourage commerce with the frontier. He was made chairman of two important committees concerned with the West.

One committee was assigned to draw up temporary governments for the western territories, to serve until the issue of statehood could be decided. The result of the committee's work was a framework for territorial government that has been used ever since by the United States. Under Monroe's plan, a territory is headed by a governor who is appointed by Congress or the President. A congressional committee governs the territory, but its citizens elect a territorial legislature to handle local government. At various times this system was used to govern many of the present states; it is still used to govern such present territories as Guam and the Virgin Islands.

A Trade Route Tussle

Monroe's second committee dealt with United States trading rights on the Mississippi River. This complicated issue affected the main artery of the western frontier. At this time, France claimed the northern part of the Mississippi and Spain the southern part. But the Americans, pushing now ever further westward into the heart of the continent, relied upon the river to ship their farm produce and furs to market — carrying goods to the East Coast over mountains and through forests was not practical. However, to use the Mississippi and especially the port of New Orleans, frontier Americans had to pay tolls and fees to the French and Spanish.

In 1785, John Jay began negotiating with Spain for a trade agreement that would greatly benefit eastern businessmen. Jay felt that it was important for the United States to open up new commercial partners among the nations of Europe. Spain wanted the United States to give up all navigation rights on the Mississippi River for 25 years in return for Spain's signature on the trade treaty. Jay, an easterner who cared little for the West, was willing to do this. But Monroe, who felt that the river highway was necessary to the development of the United States, led a group of congressmen in opposition to Jay.

Early in 1786, Monroe had made a second trip into the western territories, this time traveling to Pittsburgh and into Kentucky. From his talks with many of the frontier dwellers, he learned the importance of the Ohio and Mississippi trade routes in their lives. He felt that rights to these routes could not be signed away for the sake of eastern business interests. As a result of Monroe's opposition, Jay's commercial agreement with Spain was not signed, and the lower Mississippi remained open to American trade. But Monroe's passionate commitment to the West did not end there. More than 17 years later, the Mississippi River was to be the key feature of one of Monroe's most famous political acts.

Interstate and Foreign Commerce

Another problem occupied Monroe during his years in Congress. It was the thorny issue of commerce: who should regulate the states' trade with each other and with other countries—the individual states or the national government? Some states had negotiated individual trade agreements with England; others would not allow British goods to enter. To make matters worse, some of the states levied steep taxes on goods produced in other states. New York, for example, taxed products from the New England states. Connecticut taxed the products of other states but welcomed British goods. These individual, independent commercial considerations were leading to bad feeling between the states.

Monroe served on Congress' commerce committee. He studied the problem and decided that the central, or national, government ought to regulate the commerce of all the states. In 1785, he sponsored a bill to place control of interstate and foreign trade in the hands of the national government. He wrote to Jefferson, who was in Paris at the time: "This will give the Union an authority upon the states respectively which will last with it [and] hold it together in its present form longer than any principle it now contains." The bill was defeated by congressmen who supported the rights of the individual states. But because of his efforts on its behalf, Monroe became known as a supporter of a strong national government. Furthermore, the groundwork he laid in 1785 helped the principle of federal regulation of interstate and foreign commerce find its way into the new Constitution a few years later.

After several years in Congress, Monroe began to grow disillusioned with political life. He was idealistic, and he felt that many of his fellow congressmen spent too much time bickering over their states' interests when they should have been working together to strengthen the new nation. In addition, his uncle, Joseph Jones, who had helped Monroe get appointed as Jefferson's aide, was urging him to decide upon a life's work. A full-time political career was unheard-of in those days, especially for one so young. It was time Monroe got down to the practice of law, Jones informed him, if he ever intended to earn a living as a lawyer. So Monroe began planning to retire from Congress to a law practice in Fredericksburg. And by 1786, he had another reason to settle down and start earning a good living.

A WHIRLWIND ROMANCE

Congress met in New York City during the 1785–1786 session. Although he was busy with his congressional duties, Monroe was not too busy to sample the social life of the country's largest city. Lord Stirling, his former commanding officer,

Silhouettes cut out of black paper were a popular art form in the 19th century. Although this silhouette was made in 1830, it shows the style of dress that Monroe had preserved carefully since the late 1700s: high boots, knee breeches or tights, long coat, top hat, and ruffled shirt-collar. (James Monroe Museum and Memorial Library.)

lived in New York and was connected with many of the city's most prominent families. He introduced Monroe at teas and parties, and soon the 27-year-old Virginian became a familiar figure on the social scene.

Monroe was a distinctive figure, too — nearly six feet tall, broad-shouldered, lean and fit from his years of military service and from his lifelong love of outdoor activities. In the style of the time, he wore his hair long, tied back in a ponytail at the base of his neck. He had deep-set, dark eyes and a slight cleft in his chin, and he wore the usual male costume of high-collared coats, ruffled shirts, tight knee-breeches, and high boots.

Monroe was a particularly earnest and serious man, but he was enough of a romantic that he lost his heart to one of the most popular and beautiful society girls in New York. She was Elizabeth Kortright, the dark-haired, dark-eyed daughter of a former British army officer, and she was 10 years younger than Monroe. Although he had told friends many times that he had no intention of taking on the responsibilities of marriage and family, Monroe fell in love with Elizabeth and she with him. Their courtship was brief but intense; only a few weeks after their first meeting they became engaged.

In May of 1786, Monroe wrote to Jefferson: "You will be surprised to hear that I have formed the most interesting connection possible in human life, with a young lady in this town." Jefferson assumed that his young friend was announcing that he had fallen in love and was thinking of getting married, but in fact Monroe and Elizabeth had already been married months before, in February. They lived with Elizabeth's father until Congress ended, and then Monroe resigned from politics. He took his bride to Fredericksburg, where they moved into a house owned by Monroe's uncle Joseph. The former congressman then opened a law office and prepared for private life.

Elizabeth Kortright, a dark-eyed beauty, stole Monroe's heart in 1786. This portrait was painted by Benjamin West, an American painter who lived and worked in London. It was made during the early 1800s, when the Monroes lived in England. (Frick Art Reference Library.)

RETURN TO POLITICS

Things went well at first. Monroe had no shortage of clients, thanks to his prominent background of military and political service and to his uncle's influence. His first daughter, Eliza Kortright Monroe, was born in December; Monroe wrote to Jefferson that, although she was noisy, she was amusing. But Monroe found that he quickly grew bored with his private law practice. He missed the excitement of political life and was happy to run for the Virginia House of Delegates when friends suggested that he do so. He was easily elected.

The following year, however, brought a political disappointment. Because many Americans were displeased with the country's Articles of Confederation, a Constitutional Convention was called. It was to meet in Philadelphia and draw up a new constitution for the national government. Monroe wanted very much to be chosen for the Virginia delegation to the Constitutional Convention, but he was not. In 1788, though, he did serve on the 170-member Virginia Ratifying Convention that met in Richmond to vote on whether or not to accept the Constitution.

A Vote Against the Constitution

The delegates to the Ratifying Convention were almost evenly divided between those who liked the Constitution and those who objected to it. Madison supported it, but Patrick Henry felt it gave up too many of the states' rights. Each man had followers, but Monroe refused to ally himself with either side. He decided to study the Constitution carefully and base his vote on specific issues.

He had several strong objections to the Constitution. He didn't like the fact that the number of states needed to approve an international treaty had been reduced from nine to seven (out of 13). Under the old Articles of Confederation,

When Monroe brought his bride to Fredericksburg, Virginia, in 1786, he set up his law practice in this building. Today, it is the fifth presidential library, where Monroe's papers and items relating to his presidency are stored. (James Monroe Museum and Memorial Library.)

seven states had voted to give the Mississippi to Spain; the move was defeated, but Monroe was afraid that the new Constitution would make it possible. He also felt that the Constitution should include a statement of the individual rights for which Americans had fought in the War of Independence. This was added later to the Constitution in the form of the Bill of Rights.

All things considered, Monroe felt that the Constitution was not quite good enough and voted against it. It passed, however—but only by 10 votes. Once the Constitution had become law, even Monroe admitted that it was good to have a firm basis for national law. He expected that changes—such as the Bill of Rights—would improve the Constitution as time went on.

Political Defeat and Victory

In the fall of 1788, Monroe ran for Congress but was defeated by James Madison. It was his first—and last—defeat in an election. Although he was disappointed, he was by no means ready to give up politics.

The following year, he and his family moved to Charlottesville, in western central Virginia. The move brought Monroe closer to Jefferson's home at Monticello; this was important to both men, as their friendship and correspondence had flourished. It also brought him away from the coastal (tidewater) region of Virginia, which was heavily influenced by traditional eastern thinking. In Charlottesville, Monroe found a free-spirited climate of thought, more in tune with his own beliefs about the importance of the West and the Mississippi River. He also found an opportunity to re-enter the political arena. In 1790, Monroe ran against his old friend John Marshall for a seat in the United States Senate and was elected.

PARTY POLITICS

Just as he stayed close to Jefferson personally and geograph-ically, Monroe followed Jefferson's lead in politics. Already the growth of political parties was beginning to divide the leadership of the new republic into two groups. One group, led by Washington, became known as Federalists. Alexander Hamilton and John Adams were two important Federalists. The other group, led by Jefferson (who served as secretary of state under Washington until 1793), was called the Jeffer-sonian Republicans or the Democratic-Republicans. By the early 1790s, Madison and Monroe had become Republicans.

The chief object of the Federalists was the centralizing of power in a strong national, or federal, government. Al-though he had supported this principle at the beginning of his political career, Monroe now opposed it. Like Jefferson, he felt that the Federalists, especially Hamilton, wanted to give the central government too much power in areas like cur-rency regulation and taxation. The Republicans, on the other hand, favored states' rights.

But the biggest issue that divided the Federalists and the Republicans was the question of relationships between the United States and the European powers. This issue grew in importance during Washington's presidency as the two most powerful nations in Europe—England and France—drew closer to war. European affairs had been greatly complicated by the French Revolution in 1789.

International Politics

Although many leaders of the French Revolution claimed to have been inspired by the American War of Independence, there were several important differences between these two historic events. The American Revolution had been the act of a distant colony seeking fair treatment at first, and eventually freedom from a parent country. The French Revolution, however, was the violent and bloody overthrow of a long-established monarchy. Also, the American Revolution was brought about largely by geographic distance and the corresponding desire for economic independence; the French Revolution was a class war.

American attitudes toward events in France varied widely. Some Americans felt that the French republicans, or revolutionaries, were their brothers in arms; they also remembered with gratitude France's help during the War of Independence. Others felt that the French republicans were a dangerous, undisciplined mob. Washington's official policy was to remain completely neutral in all disputes between the European nations. Complete neutrality, however, proved impossible, and the United States found itself more and more involved in European affairs.

Hamilton, and many other Federalists, believed that it was in the best interests of the United States to rebuild strong ties with England through trade agreements and treaties. They worked to bring their point of view to bear upon Washington. Completely opposed to this were the Republicans, who ardently admired the French revolutionary spirit and wanted the United States to have strong ties with France. Because France and England were clearly headed for war, it became more and more difficult for the United States to remain neutral or to maintain good relations with both countries. Each country wanted the United States to take its side against the other.

As a Jeffersonian Republican, Monroe was an open critic of Washington's policy of cautious neutrality. He and other Republicans made no secret of the fact that they hoped Jefferson would become President when Washington stepped down. But as he carried out his senatorial duties in the temporary capital, New York, Monroe did not turn into a diehard Republican. When he disagreed with fellow Republicans, he said so. He refused to take sides along strict party lines; rather, he insisted that every issue be examined on its own merits. Needless to say, this sometimes drew down upon him the anger of other Republicans. It also attracted the respect of Washington, who admired independent thinking and hated party politics. Thus, in 1794, Washington decided that Monroe's stubborn independence, as well as his Republicanism, made him the perfect choice for a delicate diplomatic task.

Chapter 3

Two Missions to France

U nfortunately for Monroe, the very same quality of independent thinking that made Washington respect him also caused his first diplomatic mission to fail. It was so serious a failure, in fact, that it almost destroyed his entire career.

At first, however, it seemed like a big step forward—although a surprising one. In May of 1794, Secretary of State Edmund Randolph told Monroe that President Washington wanted to appoint him as the United States minister (as ambassadors were then called) to France. He would be replacing Gouverneur Morris, a Federalist politician to whom the French had taken a great dislike. Morris, for his part, took no pains hiding his distaste for the new French republic.

Jefferson and Madison shared Monroe's surprise that Washington would ask a member of the opposition party to fill an important diplomatic post. But they agreed with Monroe that the position would advance both his career and the Republican movement in general, and they advised him to accept.

In reality, Washington had several good reasons for wanting Monroe to go to France. First, the French were tired of Washington's neutrality and disgusted with Morris' Federalism. Washington felt that it would please them if someone known to be sympathetic to France were sent to replace

Morris. In addition, Washington hoped that the Republicans would be grateful for the appointment and would be less hostile to his administration; he wanted to mend the split between the two parties, if possible. Finally, he believed that Monroe, as a young politician eager to advance his career, would behave with restraint in a position that was expected to be little more than a formality.

Monroe was told that his mission was simply to repair the poor feelings that existed between France and the United States. France was currently at war with England, and the French were angry that the United States had sent a delegation under John Jay to negotiate a treaty with England. They felt that France's treaty with the United States, signed during the War of Independence, made it impossible for the United States to enter into any relationship with the English. Monroe's job was to soothe the ruffled French without really saying or doing anything of significance. But Washington had reckoned without Monroe's strong Republican feelings.

The First Mission

The new minister and his wife were settled in Paris by early August of 1794. Almost immediately, from the point of view of Washington and the Federalists at home, Monroe's mission got off on the wrong foot. He spoke to the French National Convention in praise of the republic and even embraced the president of the Convention. Hamilton and others pointed out acidly to Washington that this extremely friendly behavior did more than soothe French feelings—it actually encouraged the French to believe that the United States might side with France against England. Secretary of State Randolph sent Monroe a letter with an official reprimand, and the minister's troubles began in earnest.

While Jay's negotiations with the British continued, the French grew more and more upset. When the United States and England signed a treaty in November, the French insisted on knowing its terms. Monroe was ready to tell them, but he received strict orders not to do so. The British were furious that Monroe would even consider such a course, and Jay was equally angry. He made his displeasure clear to Washington and to Congress. Perhaps Jay remembered being opposed by Monroe years before in the Congress of the Confederation. At any rate, he and Monroe quarreled over the matter of the treaty and Jay, because he was a Federalist, had more friends in the administration to support his side of the argument than Monroe had.

Monroe struggled for more than a year and a half to pacify the French about the treaty. In fact, the treaty was mostly concerned with commercial matters and with payments to Americans for property damaged during the war. But the French were convinced that it was a military treaty that posed a threat to France. Monroe found himself in the awkward position of having to reassure his hosts that they had nothing to worry about while at the same time giving them no real information.

A Displeased Washington

As if this position were not difficult enough, Monroe became increasingly aware that he strongly disagreed with Washington's foreign policy. If he followed his instructions from Washington, he would be acting against what he believed to be the country's best interests—and, at the same time, he would alienate his friends in the Republican Party. As a result, he acted more and more as a representative of the Republican Party and less and less as a representative of Washington's administration. He even encouraged the French to believe that Jefferson would probably become President in 1796, after which French-American relations would improve. It soon became clear to Washington that Monroe was not furthering his policy in France.

Then, in 1796, the government of France announced that the treaty between the United States and England violated the French-American treaty of 1778. This meant, in the eyes of the French, that the 1778 treaty was cancelled. The French minister to the United States was called home, and France announced that it would attack any American ships that engaged in trade with England.

Back in the United States, the Federalist Party was in an uproar of indignation over what it believed was Monroe's poor handling of the situation. Washington told Congress that he was recalling Monroe and would appoint a new minister, someone who would support official government policy, not work against it. The President appointed a Federalist, Charles Cotesworth Pinckney, to the post. Washington was dismayed, however, when France announced that it would not receive any more American ministers until the United States showed that it was prepared to honor the treaty of 1778 by breaking off relations with England. Such a breaking-off of diplomatic relations would be one step short of war.

Monroe left his post in December of 1796, filled with regret at the failure of his mission and worry over his future, but he did not leave Paris. He and Elizabeth remained there for several months and also made short trips to other European capitals. In the spring, they set sail for home. Monroe prepared to return to his law practice—but he also hoped that his political career had not ended forever after the failure of his mission to France.

PROBLEMS BACK HOME

Immediately upon his return from Europe, Monroe found himself embroiled in two troublesome disputes. One was political; the other was personal, and nearly led to a duel.

The political dispute involved Monroe's standing with

the two parties. John Adams, a Federalist who had succeeded Washington as President, called Monroe "a disgraced minister, recalled in displeasure for misconduct." He and the other Federalists persisted in treating Monroe as a political has-been. On the other hand, Jefferson was Adams' Vice-President (the voting practice of the time made it possible for the top two executives of the land to belong to rival parties). He and other Republicans put forth the view that Monroe had acted in good faith in France and had been dismissed because he would not compromise his principles. Jefferson assured Monroe that, in time, his "disgrace" would be forgotten and he would return to national politics.

In the meanwhile, Monroe felt hurt and angry over his dismissal and over the suggestion that he had acted wrongly. In the winter of 1797–1798, he wrote and published a long booklet called *A View of the Conduct of the Executive, in the Foreign Affairs of the United States*. Because it was extremely critical of Washington's policy toward France, Washington never forgave Monroe for publishing the booklet, and remained cool toward his fellow Virginian for the rest of his life. Later in life, though, Monroe was to admit that his feelings about Washington, Jay, and the whole question of French policy had softened considerably.

An Angry Hamilton

Also in 1797, Monroe found himself in the middle of a delicate and embarrassing personal dispute. It concerned Alexander Hamilton, the arch-Federalist and one of Monroe's greatest political opponents. Back in 1790, Hamilton had an affair with a young married woman named Reynolds. Her husband had then blackmailed Hamilton. When the situation became known to a few people in the government, a committee was formed to carry out a private investigation. Monroe had been a member of the committee. Like the other members, Monroe was convinced that, although Hamilton had behaved foolishly, he had done nothing criminal or harmful to the government. Monroe helped to hush the matter up and then, after 1792, forgot all about it.

Suddenly, in 1797, a pamphlet exposing the whole sordid affair was published in Philadelphia. Hamilton was certain that Monroe was behind this attempt to blacken his name and drive him out of politics. He persisted in accusing Monroe of writing the pamphlet, although Monroe denied it repeatedly.

Finally, it became clear that the enraged Hamilton was trying to provoke Monroe into challenging him to a duel. Duelling was actually illegal. Moreover, public sympathy usually lay with the person challenged, not with the challenger, because it was considered a point of honor not to refuse a challenge. A mutual acquaintance explained to Hamilton that Monroe would not issue the challenge but was willing to fight if Hamilton challenged him. (It is ironic that this acquaintance was Aaron Burr, the man who would kill Hamilton in a duel seven years later.) Hamilton then let the Reynolds matter drop, although his personal and political dislike of Monroe was stronger than ever.

A MUCH-LOVED GOVERNOR

Once settled at his home in Virginia after his return from France, Monroe concentrated on building up his on-again, off-again law practice. He kept in close touch with Jefferson and other prominent political friends. He also celebrated the birth of a son in 1799. Tragically, the child was to die two years later.

Monroe had other cause for celebration in 1799. He had feared that his political career might be over, but he soon found that—at least in his home state—he was much respected and

*In 1799, the Monroes moved into a new house called
Highland, in Charlottesville, Virginia. At that time, the house
included a different structure on the left; the current two-story
section was added after Monroe's death. The Monroes lived at
Highland on and off until 1823. Today, it is maintained as a
museum by the College of William and Mary, where Monroe
went to school. (Ash Lawn-Highland.)*

honored. When he agreed to run for governor in 1799, he
found that everyone expected him to win the election. No one
would run against him. He was elected without opposition
to a one-year term and then reelected for two more terms in
the two succeeding years. He thus held the highest office in
the state in 1800, 1801, and 1802.

In a long career of public service, these three years of
governorship were exceptionally productive. Pleased to be

at work in public service again, and happy to have his self-confidence restored, Monroe seems to have thrown himself into his duties with special energy. The biggest crisis of the three years came during his first term when he suppressed a slave revolt.

A Crisis Is Avoided

The southern slave states were filled with rumors about the black leader Toussaint-Louverture, a former slave who had become a general on the Caribbean island of Hispaniola, now divided between the countries of Haiti and the Dominican Republic. Toussaint-Louverture was driving the French out of their colony of Haiti. His success inspired many slaves in the United States to plan uprisings. One such slave, named Gabriel, lived on a plantation near Richmond. He planned a revolt that was headed off when one of the plotters secretly told Monroe of the plan. The governor called out the militia, arrested the ringleaders, and stopped the uprising just hours before it began. The citizens of Virginia praised Monroe for his quick, decisive action in averting disaster, but Monroe admitted privately that the problem of slavery had only been postponed, not solved. Years later, as President, he would face the slavery issue again.

The rest of Monroe's three-year governorship was peaceful. He carried out many useful, practical programs, including a reform of the state tax system, a reorganization of the courts, and a restructuring of the militia. He built many roads and bridges, and had the Potomac and James rivers widened and cleared for shipping. Schools, hospitals, and poorhouses were built during his administration; so was the state house in Richmond (Jefferson was the building's architect).

Monroe could probably have continued as Virginia's governor for as many years as he wanted. But events in and after 1800 moved him once again in the direction of national and international politics.

One such event was the defeat of the Federalist John Adams in the election of 1800. Jefferson, the leading Republican and Monroe's mentor, was then elected President. He named Madison secretary of state. These two men made Monroe's return to diplomacy possible. Other key events in Monroe's political comeback involved France, Spain, and one of his old enthusiasms, the Mississippi River.

NAPOLEON AND THE MISSISSIPPI

Ever since the beginning of colonization in the Americas, ownership of the territories south and west of the 13 original colonies had been a confused matter. But by 1800 it seemed to have been settled. After years of claims, counterclaims, and swaps, the lands of Florida, Louisiana, and Texas belonged to King Carlos IV of Spain. Under the Treaty of San Lorenzo el Real, the United States had the right to navigate the Mississippi River. Then, in 1801, this harmonious arrangement was threatened. The United States learned that Spain was giving the entire Louisiana Territory—including the Mississippi and the port of New Orleans—to France.

This was terrible news. As Monroe had recognized years before, the river and the port were vital to trade and expansion in the western territories of the United States. France had not been on friendly terms with the United States since Monroe was dismissed as minister. Furthermore, the French republic, originally hailed by Jefferson, Monroe, and other Republicans, had undergone many changes in the past few years.

France was now ruled by Napoleon Bonaparte. Not yet Emperor, he used the title First Consul, but he ruled with imperial control and soaring ambition. The other nations of the world were well aware that Napoleon wanted to extend French power and dominion wherever possible. Even Jefferson, who had wanted the United States and France to be allies, was wary of the First Consul. He felt that Napoleon should be kept out of the Americas—otherwise, the ambitious Corsican might decide to add the United States to his list of conquests. President Jefferson feared war with France, but he also feared that the United States would have to ally itself with England to protect itself from Napoleon. "The day that France takes possession of New Orleans," he wrote in alarm, "we must marry ourselves to the British fleet and nation."

SECOND MISSION TO FRANCE

Late in 1802, Jefferson wrote to Monroe, asking him to undertake a special diplomatic mission to France. Indeed, wrote the President, so great was the need that he could not allow Monroe to refuse. The mission, as it turned out, was of staggering magnitude: it was nothing less than to buy the Louisiana Territory from Napoleon! The transaction, as well as the land involved, was to become known to history as the Louisiana Purchase.

The United States minister to France, Robert R. Livingston, had learned that Napoleon might be willing to consider selling the Territory. But although Livingston had tried for months, he had been unable to arrive at any definite terms with the First Consul. Jefferson felt that the presence of Monroe, a man who had been honored by France, would help the negotiations. Monroe's appointment as special envoy was quickly approved, and he arrived in France early in 1803. (Elizabeth accompanied her husband, along with their 16-year-old daughter Eliza and their infant daughter, Maria Hester.)

The extent of Monroe's participation in the Louisiana

Purchase is a questionable one. Napoleon finally did make a firm offer to Livingston to sell the Louisiana Territory, just two days before Monroe arrived in France. Because Livingston wanted to get the credit for making the deal, he did not immediately inform Monroe that the offer had been made. Monroe, however, soon found out about the negotiations from his French friends. After that, although he and Livingston were jealous of each other and not on very good terms, the two Americans worked together through most of April to arrange the purchase price and other details.

Napoleon's price for the Louisiana Purchase was $15 million. Both Livingston and Monroe were unsure about whether they should go ahead and make a definite deal with the First Consul. It was not the price that gave them pause but the question of whether such a purchase was legal under the United States Constitution. But they did not have the time to refer this complicated point back to Congress for approval. The volatile First Consul could change his mind at any moment.

At the same time, both men knew that the Mississippi could not be allowed to fall into the hands of a nation that might become an enemy of their country; Monroe, in particular, had always believed in the importance of the West and was eager to secure a definite title to it. The Louisiana Territory was much larger than the present state of Louisiana; in fact, it was as large as the original 13 colonies put together. So, almost without stopping to think, Livingston and Monroe agreed to Napoleon's terms. And as it turned out, the Senate later approved the Louisiana Purchase by a large majority.

The Result and the Reward

Why did Napoleon sell the Louisiana Territory? It is impossible to say for sure. But France's failure to hold onto its colony in Hispaniola may have discouraged the First Consul from

The Greatest Bargain in American History

When James Monroe and Robert Livingston signed the Louisiana Purchase Treaty, they immediately doubled the size of the United States with a few strokes of their quill pens. But the actual boundaries of the Purchase were still not completely charted. The French minister Talleyrand is said to have answered Livingston's questions about the boundaries with the polite remark, "I can give you no direction. You have made a noble bargain for yourselves, and I suppose you will make the most of it."

Everyone knew that the Mississippi River was the eastern boundary of the Louisiana Purchase and that the Rocky Mountains (then called the Stony Mountains) formed its western edge. But it was not until 1818–1819 that the precise physical boundaries for the other sides of the Purchase were worked out with Spain and England, whose colonies adjoined the Louisiana Territory on the southwest and the north, respectively.

The territory acquired for the United States by the Louisiana Purchase included all of the present states of Louisiana, Missouri, Arkansas, Iowa, South Dakota, North Dakota, Nebraska, and Oklahoma, as well as most of Kansas, Colorado, Wyoming, Montana, and Minnesota. Much of it was rich, productive farmland or pasture; it also held valuable forests and mineral resources. The 828,000 square miles of the Louisiana Purchase cost

the United States about three cents an acre.
All told, it was probably the best bargain the
United States ever made.

further expansion in the New World. In addition, France was
once again on the verge of open war with England and needed
funds with which to support the coming conflict. Napoleon
probably felt that, with war all around him in Europe, he had
little time for far-flung activities in Louisiana. Finally, it is
certain that he wanted the United States to grow larger and
stronger so that his own enemy, England, would have a power
to reckon with in North America. He is said to have remarked,
as he signed the formal treaty on May 2, 1803, "I have just
given England a maritime power that sooner or later will lay
low her pride." For his part, Livingston said, "We have lived
long, but this is the noblest work of our whole lives."

Many United States citizens shared that view. They were
proud of their country's new size and importance, and they
felt secure about its economic future. The Louisiana Purchase
gave an extra push to the steady westward flow of frontiersmen, pioneers, and settlers. It was widely regarded as a
diplomatic triumph.

Because he was present during the final negotiations and
signed his name to the treaty, Monroe received credit for helping to bring about the Louisiana Purchase. As he continued
his political career, he gradually became known as the man
who had bargained with Napoleon for the Purchase. His
friends, including Jefferson and Madison, helped to encourage
this popular idea.

Unfortunately, it was not strictly true. Livingston, the
original minister to France, actually played a greater part in

the Purchase. He had worked on it for many long months before Monroe even arrived in France. But people remembered that Monroe had gone to France and that, immediately after his arrival it seemed, the Louisiana Purchase took place. Because Livingston did not go on to a high-level career in politics, his part in the Purchase was pretty much forgotten. This widespread misunderstanding over who was really the negotiator of the Purchase was to cause some difficulties for Monroe a few years later.

In the meantime, however, he was filled with pleasure at the successful outcome of his second mission to France. At last, he felt, the "disgrace" of his first mission had been forgotten. Indeed, Jefferson promptly entrusted him with another very important diplomatic post: he named Monroe minister to England. In June of 1803, the new minister—who had already been joined in France by his family—arrived in London.

THE LEWIS AND CLARK EXPEDITION

One important outcome of the Louisiana Purchase was the Lewis and Clark Expedition. It took place from 1804 to 1806, while Monroe was attending to his new duties in London. Nevertheless, as one of the signers of the Louisiana Purchase, Monroe had helped bring the expedition into being, and surely he followed accounts of its progress with great interest and attention—as did America and the world.

The expedition was planned and authorized by President Jefferson to explore the vast new western territory that had been added to the United States by the Louisiana Purchase. Its leaders were Meriwether Lewis, Jefferson's 29-year-old secretary, and William Clark, a 33-year-old Virginian; both were army officers.

In May of 1804, Lewis and Clark set off westward from

St. Louis, Missouri, which was then a frontier town. They were accompanied by about 40 men; later they added Indian guides. On foot and by boat, they spent the following two years and four months traveling up the Missouri River to its source in Montana, across the Continental Divide in the Rocky Mountains, and down the Columbia River to the Pacific Ocean—and back again.

Their trip was the first documented overland journey by white men from the settled East Coast to the western ocean, and it was one of the greatest journeys of exploration and discovery of all time. In the face of great obstacles—hostile Indians, hunger, harsh weather, dauntingly difficult terrain, and deadly creatures such as the rattlesnake and grizzly bear—the expedition made maps and gathered a great variety of information about the lands and Indian people of the American West. Much of what they learned was completely new.

The diaries Lewis and Clark kept on their journey give us a vivid glimpse of what the Great Plains, the Rocky Mountains, and the Pacific Northwest were like before the coming of the white man. And the diaries also contain true accounts of brave people and stirring adventures.

Lewis and Clark were hailed as heroes upon their return to St. Louis in September of 1806. Not only had they brought back a wealth of scientific and geographic information, but they and the soldiers and Indians who accompanied them had opened the door to the grand new Louisiana Territory that Monroe had helped to purchase. Thousands of other travelers, traders, and settlers would soon follow in Lewis and Clark's footsteps as the wild territory gradually became part of the United States.

Chapter 4

America's Greatest Challenge

Monroe's appointment as minister to England came at a time of great tension between that country and the United States. In fact, the two nations were only a few years away from the War of 1812 — a war that would come close to bringing the United States to its knees.

But Monroe knew nothing of this in 1803. As the United States minister to England, he hoped to improve relations between the two countries. He realized that the job would be a difficult one; he only hoped it would not prove to be impossible.

The United States was growing increasingly angry with England over its actions on the high seas. The most infuriating British practice was called impressment: a cruel way of forcing men into military service. Years of intermittent war with France had left the British Royal Navy starving for manpower, and it used any means at hand to put men to work on its ships. Roving bands of agents, called press gangs, descended upon British towns and actually kidnapped any able-bodied men who could not elude them. These men were then taken aboard navy vessels and forced to sign into service. Because most of the victims of the press gangs were poor and illiterate, many well-to-do members of society saw nothing wrong in this military abduction. Press gangs were one of the terrors of life for England's lower class for many years.

PRESS GANGS FROM ABROAD

As bad as the practice of impressment was, the British could have carried on impressing their own men in their own country for years and not made the United States angry. But it was a different matter when the British began forcibly impressing Americans. Sailors whose ships stopped at British ports were in danger of being seized in public, in broad daylight, from inns, taverns, or simply as they walked down the street. Even worse was England's policy of impressment on the high seas.

Well-armed British navy frigates roamed international waters, ordering American ships to halt and submit to searches. At first, the British claimed to be looking for deserters from the Royal Navy. True, there were many deserters, since conditions in the navy were dreadful; in fact, many deserters did indeed sign on to American ships, hoping to start new lives in the United States. Soon, however, it became a common practice for the British to seize anyone on board a ship who had a British accent—even American citizens. They also confiscated ships' cargoes and sometimes entire vessels on the charge of aiding deserters.

At the heart of the impressment issue was the fact that it gave England a chance to treat the United States as though it were still a colony, not a separate sovereign state. They thus treated Americans as though they were subject to British law. One particularly sore point was the question of whether British citizens could become United States citizens. England said never: once a British citizen, always a British citizen. But under United States law, it was possible for a citizen of any country to be naturalized as an American citizen. As a result, former British citizens who were now American sailors were being routinely impressed by the British during their searches.

Sitting Ducks on the High Seas

Because the American ships were mostly slow, unarmed merchant vessels, they had no choice but to submit to these searches and seizures at the hands of the British; American sea captains who resisted were fired upon and quickly subdued. But Americans deeply resented the high-handed, often brutal methods used by the British. They claimed that searches and impressment were illegal in international waters. Even more, they resented the insult to American dignity and independence. One sovereign nation, Americans said, should not be treated this way by another, especially since the two countries were not at war.

Dozens of official protests were sent by Presidents Washington, Adams, and Jefferson to London, but the British simply refused to discuss the issue. They regarded impressment as their right and as a way of putting the rebellious colonies in their place. Although there seemed little the United States could do about it, American outrage toward England steadily grew. By the time Monroe arrived to take up his post in London, impressment had become one of the major issues in world politics.

Monroe worked hard on behalf of those Americans who had suffered as a result of impressment. He personally handled many cases of wrongful imprisonment, intervening whenever possible and freeing his countrymen. He also spent much time and energy pursuing American claims for property confiscated or damaged during searches. Most of all, however, he tried to get the British government to change its policy—but with no success. His requests were met with bland refusals. After the excitement of the Louisiana Purchase, Monroe found his time in London to be politically frustrating. It was also financially difficult.

MONEY TROUBLES

All through his adult life, Monroe had alternated between working as a private citizen and holding public office. Many other men of his time did the same. Most, however, found it impossible to live on their government salaries. Those who did not have large private incomes ran into money trouble sooner or later. Monroe was not a rich man, and periodic financial difficulties haunted him from the 1790s onward.

Monroe had sold his share of the family estate in Westmoreland County years earlier. When he moved to Charlottesville in 1789, he planned to operate a large plantation on his land there. But his frequent long absences on government service caused the farm to suffer; before long, he realized that it would never be a source of income. Similarly, his law practice suffered because he never devoted himself to it for more than a year or so at a time. By the time of his first mission to France, he had turned most of his legal work over to colleagues. Monroe tried to make his livelihood as a public servant, but he was to discover, too late, that this was a tragic mistake.

During his years in London, his salary was about $9,000 a year. This would have been enough to permit a lavish lifestyle at home, but in Europe it was not enough to support a ministry in the required style. Monroe was forced to borrow money from Secretary of State Madison, who was comfortably wealthy.

In addition to money worries, Monroe and Elizabeth found their social life in London disappointing. They had been extremely popular in Paris; Elizabeth once remarked that she had been cheered in public every time she went to the theater there. But London society snubbed the Monroes, for several reasons.

One reason was that, although Monroe had grown a great deal more critical of the French over the years, he was still remembered by the British as a man with pro-French, anti-British leanings. Another reason was that Elizabeth Monroe was no longer the popular, vivacious girl who had captured Monroe's heart in New York. She had matured into a somewhat reserved woman; in addition, she was not in the best of health. She did not entertain or court society the way she might once have done.

But the most likely reason for the Monroes' cool reception in London was his mission – and the poor state of affairs between England and the United States in general. Monroe insisted on talking about impressment; his hosts refused. Then, to make matters worse, war between England and France broke out again. Monroe found himself awkwardly trying to tread the narrow path of neutrality between the two hostile countries.

DRIFTING TOWARD WAR

In January of 1805, Jefferson sent Monroe to Madrid, Spain. Once again he was serving as a special envoy. His mission was to help Charles Cotesworth Pinckney, the American minister to Spain, settle some questions about the boundaries of the Louisiana Purchase that adjoined Spanish territory in Florida and Texas. In addition, Monroe was to negotiate for the purchase of Florida from Spain.

Monroe found affairs in Spain to be almost as bad as those in England. Pinckney had insulted the Spanish foreign minister, who in turn was rude to Monroe. The two Americans tried to convince the Spaniard that West Florida was really part of the Louisiana Purchase and therefore should be given up to the United States. Spain, however, would not accept this argument and would not even discuss selling Florida. In May, a frustrated Monroe returned to London. There he found a situation that had gone from bad to worse.

Napoleon, who in 1804 had himself crowned Emperor of France, never made any secret of the fact that he wanted to conquer England, or at least to diminish British power and prestige. By the time Monroe returned to London, the British and French were once again at war, and now the United States was being drawn into the conflict.

An Uneasy Neutrality

England passed new laws allowing British ships to capture any vessel on the high seas that might be carrying goods to France. These laws struck a dagger-blow at American merchant trade. Not just the ships bound for France were seized; any ship that had even stopped at a French port anywhere — in the Caribbean, for example — was subject to the British laws. The ships and their cargoes were treated as prizes of war, and the profits from selling them went to line British pockets. On top of the problem of impressment, these new seizure laws gave rise to such bad feeling that Monroe began to fear the possibility of war between England and the United States. This fear would become a reality within a few years.

Back in Washington, President Jefferson planned to steer a neutral course between the two warring nations. He still carried strong feelings of sympathy for France, although even he was forced to recognize that the Emperor Napoleon I did not possess the ideals Jefferson had admired in the revolutionary republicans of 1789. Jefferson also wanted a peaceful settlement of the troubles between England and the United States. He instructed Monroe to work on a treaty with England, and he sent William Pinckney to London as a special envoy to assist him.

The European Embargo

While Monroe and Pinckney were pressing for treaty negotiations, England and France seemed to be doing their best to drag the United States into the war. Napoleon issued a statement called the Berlin Decree, which said that any American ship trading with England could be seized by France. The purpose of the decree was to destroy British commerce. England countered with a proclamation called Lord Howick's Orders, which said that any ship trading with France or its allies (Italy, Germany, and Spain) could be seized by England. Ships were safe only if they first entered a British port for purposes of trade. These orders were designed to protect British commerce.

In effect, France said to the world: "No trade with England," and England said: "No trade with Europe except through me." Obviously, an American ship could not obey both countries. The United States would be forced to take sides with one of the warring nations or else give up European trade entirely.

Still trying to remain neutral in the Napoleonic Wars, Jefferson chose to give up European trade. He hoped that by doing so he could cause England and France enough hardship that they would revoke their harsh laws. Therefore, in 1807, Congress passed an act that forbade American ships to trade with either England or France. Sadly, however, this embargo hurt American farmers and merchants much more than it hurt the British and French.

A Treaty Rejected

Meanwhile, Monroe and Pinckney had finally hammered out a treaty with representatives of the British government. From the American point of view, it was still grossly unsatisfactory. It dealt with tariffs (trade fees and taxes) and other minor matters, but it did not touch on the biggest issue of all, impressment.

The Monroe-Pinckney Treaty was sent back to the United States for approval in late 1806. Jefferson was so disappointed with it that he did not even send it to Congress. Nor did he call Monroe home or reprimand him. Perhaps he felt that this treaty was the best that could be expected under the circumstances. At any rate, the treaty was never approved, and Monroe's relationship with his old mentor began to cool.

A few months after Jefferson rejected the treaty, an incident occurred that marked the end of Monroe's service in London—and the beginning of the drift toward the War of 1812. A British cruiser, the H.M.S. *Leopard,* ordered the U.S.S. *Chesapeake* to stop and submit to a search for British deserters. When the captain of the *Chesapeake* refused, the *Leopard* attacked and destroyed the American ship. On behalf of the United States, Monroe protested in strong terms to the British government. Lord George Canning, the British foreign minister, firmly replied that the principle of impressment was not open for discussion, and that was that.

England made it clear that no further treaty negotiations or even discussions would be fruitful. Monroe was exhausted, worried about family finances, and convinced that he could accomplish nothing more in London. He asked to be relieved, and Jefferson was happy to comply. The Monroes returned to the United States in late 1807. They visited Washington before returning home, but President Jefferson was not willing to see Monroe. More than just the unsatisfactory treaty had now come between the two men.

PARTY FEUDS

The old division between the Federalist and the Republican parties had pretty much vanished from American politics, because Federalism had ceased to be a powerful force after the presidency of John Adams. But a new split arose within the Republican Party itself.

On one side were Jefferson and his close followers, including Madison. Their primary position—like Washington's had been years earlier—was that the United States should remain neutral in the European wars and should avoid war on its own account if possible. On the other side was a group of Republicans who had grown tired of Jefferson's pro-French position and felt that it was time for new thinking in the White House.

This opposition group included the so-called "War Hawks": Henry Clay of Kentucky, John C. Calhoun of South Carolina, and other politicans from the western and southern states. These fiery-tempered senators and congressmen were especially indignant about European insults to American pride. They wanted the United States to declare war on France, or on England—maybe on both. One possible reason they were so eager for war was that most of them were young; they had not suffered through the War of Independence as Jefferson, Madison, and Monroe had.

Murmurs of Candidacy

This splinter group of Republicans, joined by a few former Federalists after their party broke up, adopted Monroe as their leader, although he was in England at the time and had little connection with party politics at home. Some of them even began to speak of Monroe as a likely candidate for President in the election of 1808. This would mean that he would run against Madison, Jefferson's clear choice as a successor. The fact that his own party set Monroe up as his rival embarrassed and angered Jefferson. Together with the fiasco of the Monroe-Pinckney Treaty, this drove a wedge between the two men.

On several occasions, Monroe protested that he had no desire to become involved in party disputes. He even said that such a position made it difficult for him to do his job as minister—which, after all, required him to work for Jefferson. But the War Hawks liked Monroe for his lifelong cham-

Eliza, the older of the Monroes' two daughters, married George Hay in 1808. She and her husband made their home with the Monroes for many years. (Library of Congress.)

pionship of the West, and the other anti-Jeffersonians knew that his administrative abilities and his popularity with the people would make him a good leader. It is not clear how hard Monroe tried to patch up his growing estrangement from Jefferson, since clearly the prospect of political leadership must have been attractive to a man who had spent most of his life in government service.

Monroe did not run for President in 1808, wishing to remain on friendly terms with Madison, who was elected. Also, he may have realized that he did not have enough support to win. He had hoped, however, that Madison would make him secretary of state, but he was disappointed. Madison named instead a staunch, pro-French Jeffersonian named Robert Smith for the post. But Monroe was not out of political life for long. In 1810, he was once again elected to the Virginia legislature, and late in that year he was elected governor of Virginia for the fourth time. His term was to run through 1811, but he served only until November. War—the war with England that Monroe had feared for years—took him from the governor's mansion in Richmond to the President's Cabinet in Washington.

THE WAR THAT ALMOST WASN'T

While Monroe had been serving his state as a legislator and governor, trouble had been brewing between the United States and England. Impressment had continued unabated, despite a constant storm of American protests. To make matters worse, William Pinckney, who had succeeded Monroe as minister to England, abandoned his post in mid-1811. Although the British were insulted by this breaking-off of formal diplomatic relations, it was a naval attack that really destroyed diplomatic relations.

Punch and Counterpunch

Around the time Pinckney was leaving London, a British frigate, the *Guerriere,* had stopped the *Spitfire,* an American ship, and impressed an American sailor into the Royal Navy. Soon afterward, the American ship *President* sighted a British ship. Thinking it was the *Guerriere,* the *President* pursued and fired on the other ship in revenge for the impressment. Only after it had almost been destroyed did the *President* discover that the British ship was not the *Guerriere;* it was the *Little Belt,* which had not been involved in the original incident.

Now the British accused the Americans of aggression. The two nations were supposed to start a new session of treaty discussions, but they were off to an unpromising beginning. Members of Congress began to speak openly of war and of British piracy. President Madison still hoped that the United States could come to a peaceful agreement with England. But he realized that his secretary of state, Robert Smith, was not capable of handling such a delicate task. He asked Monroe to take over the post, which was the highest in the Cabinet.

Recall to Service

Suddenly, Monroe's moderation and his separation from the previous administration's pro-French policies were advantages. Madison probably also hoped that his appointment of Monroe would please Monroe's supporters within the Republican Party. It did heal the breach between Monroe and Madison and Jefferson.

For his part, Monroe was more than willing to assume the office he had wanted all along, even though he expressed the view that a peaceful settlement of differences with England seemed unlikely. He moved to Washington and entered one of the most grueling, challenging periods of his life.

By the time Monroe was made secretary of state, war

was just around the corner. The United States was furious to find out that the British were providing guns and ammunition to Tecumseh and other Indian leaders on the frontier so that they could attack American settlements. The War Hawks, in particular, wanted to attack the British along the northwest frontier. The stage was set for confrontation.

Then the wily Napoleon, hoping to embroil England in a war with the United States, pretended to cancel the Berlin Decree. Madison thereupon expected England to cancel Lord Howick's Orders, the proclamation which said that trade with France or its allies could only be carried on by ships that first paid taxes at British ports. The British failed to do so, and Madison urged Congress to declare war on England in June of 1812. The declaration of war was signed on June 18. It is one of the great ironies of United States history that, just two days before, England had indeed cancelled Lord Howick's Orders.

The War at Home

If the telegraph or telephone had existed in 1812, the War of 1812 would not have happened. But, by the time word of England's concession had reached the United States, the fighting was already underway. And once the battle had been joined, neither side was willing to give up until the outcome was settled on the battlefield. The Americans were determined to win, but they were badly outnumbered and ill-equipped, just as they had been in the War of Independence. In the War of 1812, the last war against another country fought on American soil, the young United States faced the greatest challenge of its 36 years.

The first fighting was in the north, near the Great Lakes and along the Canadian frontier. The United States fared badly in the early months. Detroit fell to the British, and American attempts to invade Canada through Niagara failed. But in 1813, the Americans began to score victories: the U.S.S. *Constitution* captured the *Guerriere* in the Atlantic, Oliver Perry destroyed the British fleet on Lake Erie, and William Henry Harrison led U.S. troops to victory over a combined British and Indian force at the Battle of the Thames in Ontario (Tecumseh, the famous Indian chief, was killed in this battle). The Americans also burned some British public buildings in Toronto—an act for which they would pay dearly a year later.

Monroe's duties as secretary of state were actually diminished by the outbreak of war, because diplomacy and negotiation had given way to battle. It had been more than 30 years since he retired from military service, but his fighting instincts were still strong. He wanted to return to command, raise an army, and join the action in the north. But, as often happens in political life, the past rose up to interfere with his desires.

An Old Grudge and Bad Judgment

John Armstrong, Madison's secretary of war, was the brother-in-law of Robert Livingston. Armstrong disliked Monroe because he felt that Monroe had stolen the glory that should have been Livingston's for making the Louisiana Purchase. Armstrong refused Monroe's request for command, and Monroe was left to cool his heels in Washington.

Meanwhile, Armstrong botched the conduct of the war badly. He assigned command to several incompetent officers and served as a general himself. Under his direction, the American forces suffered a series of bitter defeats on the northern front. Then came the most wretched moment of the war. A British naval force took the offensive off the eastern seaboard and ranged up and down the Chesapeake Bay area, shelling and burning. As the British drew closer to Washington, it appeared clear that the nation's capital was threatened.

The Capital in Flames

It was then that Armstrong made his greatest error in judgment. He persuaded Madison that the British were heading for Baltimore, not Washington, and that the capital did not require defenses. As a result, only 250 militiamen were left in the city. Monroe warned Madison that the British would march on Washington, but by then it was too late to mount an effective defense. On August 24, 1814, British troops marched into the streets of the United States capital. In revenge for the burnings in Toronto, they put Washington's public buildings — including the White House and the Capitol — to the torch. Madison, Monroe, and other government leaders fled the capital just hours before the British arrived, clutching bags of important state papers. The American public blamed Madison and Armstrong for this disaster but realized that Monroe had done his best to warn and protect the capital.

After three days, the British moved on to Baltimore. Although they fired shells at this city all night, they were unable to capture it. (During the bombing of Baltimore, Francis Scott Key wrote "The Star-Spangled Banner," which became the national anthem of the United States.) By this time, Armstrong had been dismissed by President Madison, who then asked Monroe to do double duty as secretary of war *and* secretary of state until the war was over.

For weeks at a stretch during the final months of 1814, Monroe did not go home or even go to bed. He merely snatched a few hours' sleep on a couch in his office from time to time. Working with Madison and other leaders, he strove mightily to keep the United States from defeat. He took charge of recruiting drives, troop assignments, promotions, dispatches from the field of battle and from abroad, and the day-to-day administration of the armed forces. He began a reorganization of the War Department for greater efficiency,

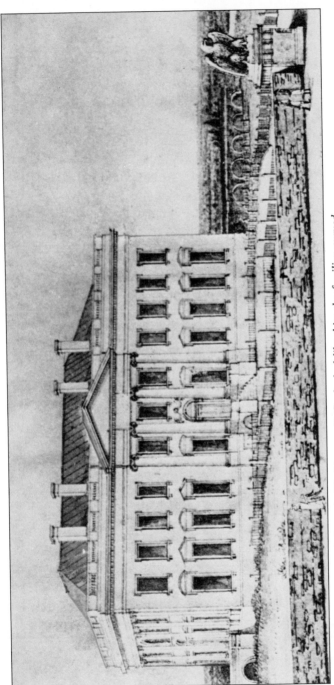

Around 1810, the President's home in Washington, D.C., looked like this; the familiar curved front portico was not added until 1829. It was made of pale-gray limestone. When the British invaded the capital in 1814, they set fire to the White House. The fire blackened the stone, and later the damage was covered with white paint. Eventually, the building came to be known as the White House—thanks to the British and their torches. (White House Historical Association.)

but his biggest problem was money. The country was bankrupt and had nothing with which to pay its soldiers. The situation was desperate. The British seemed to be winning on all fronts. They now had a force in the Gulf of Mexico and were expected to attack New Orleans at any moment.

Near the end of that year, England let the United States know that it would be willing to end the war—if certain terms were met. These terms were highly favorable to England, of course. The Americans had to give the British navigation rights on the Mississippi, all fishing rights in the banks off the Canadian coast, and part of northern Maine. But Madison and Monroe knew that the United States could not fight much longer. They sent negotiators to Ghent, in Brussels, to work out the details of a peace treaty.

Peace with a Last Twist

While negotiations were taking place in Ghent, the British force in the Gulf of Mexico moved toward New Orleans. Monroe warned Major General Andrew Jackson, who was in charge of defending Louisiana, to expect an attack. As it happened, the same time lag that had prevented the Americans from receiving news from England until after they had declared war now prevented the British from receiving important news from Ghent. On December 24, 1814, the peace treaty was signed. But Sir Edward Pakenham, the British commander in the Gulf, had heard nothing of this when he attacked New Orleans on January 8, 1815.

The Battle of New Orleans was a great victory for the United States—even though it took place after the war had technically ended. Jackson and his followers successfully defended the city and inflicted heavy losses on the enemy. This final triumph made it easier for Americans to live with their war losses. The war had accomplished nothing for the United States, and its end was greeted with relief all over the

A Pirate Among the Patriots

When Andrew Jackson led his troops against Pakenham's British army in the historic Battle of New Orleans in January of 1815, he was joined by an unlikely ally: Jean Lafitte, a notorious pirate and smuggler who ruled the Gulf of Mexico south of New Orleans, but who carried deeply patriotic feelings for the United States.

Lafitte's early life is a mystery. He was probably born in 1780, which means that he was 35 years old at the time of the battle. He entered American history in about 1810. When the Spanish South American colony of Colombia declared its independence, Lafitte obtained a privateer's commission from the Colombian government in the capital city of Cartagena. (A privateer was rather like a legal pirate, with a license to plunder enemy ships on behalf of the sponsoring country.)

Lafitte and his followers preyed upon Spanish shipping in the Gulf of Mexico. They also enriched the New Orleans economy by smuggling their loot into the city and illegally selling it to local merchants. For four years Lafitte was the leader of a colony of pirates and smugglers based in a region called Barataria, south of New Orleans. But Lafitte claimed loyalty to the United States, and the Baratarians never molested American ships.

Then, as the War of 1812 raged on, the British offered Lafitte $30,000 and a captaincy in the Royal Navy if he would help them capture New Orleans. He not only refused, but also warned U.S. officials of the danger. Unfortunately, the local government did not believe Lafitte. Instead, it sent a detachment of troops to Barataria to attack his colony. Though the Baratarians did lose a few ships, their business of piracy and smuggling continued.

In spite of the country's disappointing lack of faith in him, Lafitte remained a friend of the United States. Seeing that a tremendous battle was brewing, he offered his services to Major General Andrew Jackson. He would help Jackson defend New Orleans from the British if Jackson would grant full pardon to him and all his men. Jackson wisely agreed. The Baratarians took charge of the artillery during the Battle of New Orleans and fought with bravery and distinction. Their contribution may have saved the city. Afterward, President Madison publicly pardoned Lafitte and his men.

Lafitte was now a public hero and could have lived out his life as a respectable citizen. But piracy seemed to be in his blood. In 1817, he and 1,000 followers occupied the Gulf island that is now the site of Galveston, Texas. From there he continued to attack Spanish ships. Some of the other privateers began to vie for leadership, however, and several of them disobeyed his orders and attacked American vessels. By 1821, it was clear that the United States government would have to do something to end piracy in the Gulf.

At this point, Lafitte and his most loyal men manned his favorite ship, the *Pride*. They sailed off to an unknown fate. Lafitte's later life and death are as obscure as his early years, but he rates an interesting place in American history as the proud but piratical defender of New Orleans.

---

country. William Henry Harrison, Oliver Perry, and Andrew Jackson emerged as popular heroes. So, too, did James Monroe, who had fought as hard in Washington as any commander in the field.

Chapter 5

The Era of Good Feeling

A
s the presidential election of 1816 approached, it became clear that Monroe would most likely be chosen by his party and by the people. He had the necessary experience in administration and politics. He had shown himself to be exceptionally capable and hard-working. He had won the admiration of the American public, which regarded him as the man who had saved the United States in the War of 1812. And he was respected by most other men in government.

There were those, however, who opposed Monroe – not as an individual, but because he was a Virginian. Washington, Jefferson, and Madison had all been from Virginia, and all had served two terms as President. John Adams of Massachusetts, the second President, was the only President who was not from Virginia, and he had served only one term. Monroe was seen by some people, especially in the New England states, as the next member of the "Virginia dynasty." These people felt that the old plantation families of Virginia had controlled the presidency for too long. They wanted a change.

AN EARNED VICTORY

In 1816, however, there simply were no qualified, well-known candidates to run against Monroe, and those who opposed

Although Monroe moved away from Highland in the early years of his presidency and sold it in 1823, many of his possessions have been returned there. This bed, now in the Ash Lawn bedchamber, was carved for the Monroes in 1815. The room reflects the tasteful but simple style that Monroe favored all his life. (Ash Lawn-Highland.)

the "Virginia dynasty" had no one better to propose. Monroe first defeated William H. Crawford for the Republican nomination, and then he easily defeated Rufus King, the candidate of the fast-fading Federalist Party, in the electoral college. The fifth President of the United States would be James Monroe, with Daniel D. Tompkins of New York serving as his Vice-President.

Monroe was sworn into office on March 4, 1817. A crowd of 8,000 citizens lined the streets around Capitol Hill in Washington to watch him ride to the Capitol. Because the large marble Capitol building was still undergoing repairs of the damage it had suffered in the War of 1812, the ceremony was held in a smaller brick building that was serving as a temporary Capitol. The largest room in the building, the chamber of the House of Representatives, proved too small to hold all of the dignitaries who wanted to be present at Monroe's inauguration. Monroe therefore took the oath of office on an outside porch, in public view, and started a tradition of outdoor inaugurations that has lasted to this day.

Home Away from Home

Like the Capitol, the White House was still under repair. The Monroes continued to live in the modest house they had used as a Washington residence during the war. In the meantime, they moved their family home from Highland, the Charlottesville estate, to a new estate called Oak Hill, in Loudoun County, Virginia. Jefferson had designed the house, which was large enough for Monroe and Elizabeth, their daughter Eliza and her husband George Hay, their younger daughter Maria, and plenty of servants and guests. Monroe loved Oak Hill; sadly, however, he was not to enjoy much time there.

The Monroes spent most of their time in Washington. Elizabeth, by now in poor health, brought on the displeasure of some Washington wives by failing to entertain on the lavish scale of the last First Lady, Dolley Madison. White House events during the Monroe years tended to be rather simple, informal affairs—afternoon receptions, for example, at which a dandified foreign minister might rub elbows with an Indian chieftain in full native regalia.

The President's unpretentious social life matched his habits and appearance. He prided himself on being a plain, humble, and rather old-fashioned man. At a time when trousers were becoming standard wear for men, Monroe always dressed in the frock coat, knee breeches, and buckled shoes that had been in fashion during his youth. His clothes were of quiet, good quality but never stylish or luxurious. He wore his hair in a neat pigtail, as he had done all his life, even though many men were wearing their hair shorter by 1817. And he often wore an old-fashioned hat with a small cockade (feather ornament) in a style that had been popular among Virginians during the Revolution. For this reason, he is sometimes called "the last of the cocked-hat Presidents." The people liked their President's image: it emphasized his down-to-earth, practical qualities and it reminded them of the part he had played in the founding of the country.

THE GRAND TOUR

One of Monroe's first actions as President was to appoint a secretary of state. It had become something of a tradition that the secretary of state would have a good chance of becoming the next President; indeed, Monroe himself had done so. Therefore, the choice was an important one and the position was much coveted by anyone with presidential ambitions.

Henry Clay wanted to be Monroe's secretary of state, but the President felt it was important to appoint someone from New England, in order to appease those who feared that the South had too much power in the government. He

Gilbert Stuart, a painter who specialized in portraying public figures, became famous for his many portraits of George Washington and other Presidents. This rather formal painting shows Monroe in his official role as President. (The Metropolitan Museum of Art, bequest of Seth Low, 1929.)

asked John Quincy Adams, the son of former President John Adams, to serve. Adams was a skilled and experienced diplomat and made a very good secretary of state. Clay was disappointed, however. He managed to become Speaker of the House of Representatives and often opposed Monroe's policies during the coming years.

In June of 1817, Monroe set forth on a sweeping presidential tour of the United States, which now consisted of 19 states and the western territories. He could not visit the entire country, so he decided to concentrate on the northern areas of the East Coast, where his support was weakest. His purpose in making the trip—and throughout his entire presidency—was to try to bring the various states, regions, and factions of the country together to work for the good of the nation as a whole. This philosophy of national feeling got off to a good start during the tour.

As secretary of war, Monroe had ordered a series of forts and outposts built along the East Coast. In his inauguration speech, he said that a strong army, navy, and defense system were essential to America's security. He thus began the tour by visiting many of the coastal forts, starting with Fort McHenry, which had successfully resisted the British during the attack on Baltimore. From Baltimore he traveled through Delaware to Philadelphia. There he visited the navy yard, the hospital, and several of that city's many art exhibitions.

His next stop was Trenton, where he had been wounded 40 years before in the Battle of Trenton. He was greeted by peals of church bells and a thunderous artillery salute. Next came 10 days in New York, complete with bands, parades, steamboat rides in the harbor, and speeches. He revisited the site of the Battle of Harlem Heights and took a boat up the Hudson River to see the fort at West Point. Then it was on to Connecticut, Massachusetts (where he spent six busy days in Boston), New Hampshire, Vermont, and upstate New York. Detroit, on the eastern edge of the large Northwest Territory, was at the end of the tour. The village of Frenchtown, on the Lake Erie shore south of Detroit, was renamed Monroe during the presidential visit. Monroe returned to Washington in September; the White House had been repaired, and the Monroes moved into it.

A New Unity

Monroe's grand tour was tremendously successful and made him more popular than ever with the public. Everywhere he went, even in the former Federalist strongholds of New England, he was greeted with enthusiasm by common people and political leaders alike. His impartial interest in everything he saw, together with his calm encouragement to everyone that they share a national point of view, created an atmosphere of goodwill and cooperation not seen since the struggle for independence.

The trip accomplished what Monroe had hoped it would: it made the people feel that party rivalries were a thing of the past and that the United States was unified under a leader who represented everyone. One Boston newspaper said of Monroe's visit that it had ushered in an "era of good feeling." Monroe liked the phrase and often repeated it, and it has since been used to describe the overall tone of his presidency.

SOUTH OF THE BORDER

Monroe's first term as President was nearly evenly divided between international affairs and activities within the United States. By far, the most important of the international matters involved Spain and Florida.

Florida was a Spanish possession, and this fact had troubled Monroe for many years. As long ago as the Louisiana Purchase, he had hoped that the United States would be able to buy Florida from Spain. He felt uneasy at having a potential enemy entrenched on the southern doorstep of the country, and he believed that Spain's poor administration in Florida endangered the lives and property of American citizens in the neighboring states.

The danger to Americans came from several sources. The Seminole Indians of Florida and the Creek Indians along the Georgia-Florida border were hostile to the United States and resented having to give up their ancestral lands. Spain did not maintain enough forts or troops in Florida to control the Indians, who frequently raided into Georgia. In retaliation, U.S. troops in Georgia would strike against Indian settlements; the Indians would then retaliate with a massacre of Americans, and the violence increased.

The general lawlessness of the Florida territory made it an attractive haven for non-Indian troublemakers, too. In the summer of 1817, a band of European adventurers seized Amelia Island, a small island near the Georgia-Florida border. They attempted to set up a tiny independent republic but fought among themselves; they also raided the nearby settlements. Soon pirates, criminals, and runaway slaves made Amelia Island into an outlaw haven.

A General Causes Trouble

Monroe wanted to clean the outlaws out of Amelia Island and to restore order along the troubled Georgia-Florida border. His protests to Spain accomplished nothing, however. Therefore, in early 1818, Monroe took a bold step. He sent General Andrew Jackson to Florida with orders to clean up the border area—but *not* to attack any Spanish posts. Although this mission succeeded beyond Monroe's expectations, it also caused problems that were to haunt him years later.

Jackson felt that the United States should simply seize

Florida by force and argue about it with the Spanish later. He wrote to Monroe offering to do this, but Monroe did not write back. Later, the President would say that he never actually read the letter but turned it over to some Cabinet members. Jackson did receive some encouragement, however, possibly from John Calhoun, the secretary of war. Jackson later claimed that a man named John Rhea had delivered a message from Monroe, telling him to proceed with the conquest of Florida. But no one was ever able to identify John Rhea, and the question of how far Jackson exceeded his orders was never fully answered.

For Jackson did indeed capture Florida. He drove out the Spanish governor and set up several large American forts. Unfortunately, at the very time that Jackson was hoisting the American flag over the Florida swamps, John Quincy Adams was on the verge of signing a diplomatic treaty that would have given Florida to the United States peacefully.

When word of Jackson's activities spread, the treaty negotiations fell apart. Spain accused the United States of an act of war. England, always eager to get involved in American politics, protested that two British citizens had been killed in the fighting (they were mercenaries who had been training the Indians to fight against the whites). And Monroe was greatly disturbed and embarrassed by Jackson's excessive zeal.

He stood behind Jackson in public, though, and explained to the world that Jackson had acted in defense of American lives. Privately, he wrote to Jackson and explained, in the gentlest of terms, that the general had gone too far. Jackson's response was formal and unfriendly; he claimed that he had openly been following orders. Jackson remained angry despite the President's public support, but Monroe let the matter drop. The mystery of John Rhea was forgotten for the next few years.

Meanwhile, the United States returned the Spanish forts

in Florida to Spain while still keeping its own troops and forts there. Then, treaty negotiations resumed in 1819. Although the negotiations moved slowly because of Spain's preoccupation with its other colonies in Central and South America, they were eventually settled, with terms favorable to the United States. By early 1821, both nations had ratified a treaty that gave Florida and the Gulf of Mexico coast between Florida and Louisiana to the United States. Though Florida did not become a state until 1845, the credit for adding it to the union goes to Monroe's administration.

DOMESTIC AFFAIRS

In addition to the acquisition of Florida, Monroe's first term was marked by several other important domestic events. Many of these events were part of the nation's growth and westward expansion.

Just a few months after Monroe took office, construction of the Erie Canal began. The canal was a massive piece of engineering, designed to promote commerce between New England and the Northwest Territory. Monroe, who had always believed it was America's destiny to open up the West, supported the construction of the canal against its opponents in Congress.

Monroe's administration was a time of great technological advancement, especially in the areas of building and travel. The old sailing ships that had plied the world's waterways for centuries began to be replaced by sleek new steamships, first on the rivers and then at sea. In 1819, the first steamship to cross the ocean, the *Savannah*, left Georgia for Europe. Before the *Savannah* made its historic crossing, it carried President Monroe and several friends and Cabinet members on an all-day excursion along the Georgia coast.

Westward by Water

The building of the Erie Canal across New York State was one of the great events of early America and of Monroe's presidency. Construction work on the canal was begun in 1817, Monroe's first year in office, and was completed in 1825, his final year as President.

At the close of the 18th century, Americans were eager to push westward from the increasingly crowded eastern seaboard into the fertile valleys and plains of the Ohio Valley. But they were hampered by the enormous difficulty of travel. Between the East and the Midwest were many mountain ranges and unexplored areas. Roads were almost nonexistent; those that did exist were often nothing more than narrow trails through forests and over mountains. It was clear that if trade and settlement were to prosper in the Ohio Valley, a better travel route would have to be found or built.

In the early years of the 19th century, a group of New Yorkers developed a plan for a canal to connect the cities of Albany and Troy on the Hudson River (as well as the port of New York City, also on the Hudson) to the city of Buffalo on the shores of Lake Erie. They believed that such a canal, which would lie entirely inside New York State, would offer a swift and safe water route westward to the Great Lakes.

From Lake Erie, of course, ships could easily reach the other Great Lakes, which would then carry them as far west as present-day Michigan, Illinois, Wisconsin, and Minnesota. The federal government, however, declined to pay for the canal because many citizens preferred the idea of a turnpike road at a more southerly location. But New York State decided not to give up the idea, so the canal was built and paid for solely by New Yorkers.

The 363-mile canal was built entirely by manpower and horsepower, at a cost of about $20,000 a mile. Much of it was dug by hand, with picks and shovels. For the most part, the canal was laid at sea level, along the valley of the Mohawk River. The terrain was wild, sparsely settled, and desolate, especially the large area known as the Montezuma Swamp, which the canal had to cross.

Between Troy and Buffalo, the elevation of the land rises about 500 feet, so 82 locks were required along the length of the canal to raise and lower barges and boats to different levels. In some places, the workers had to blast through solid rock outcroppings with nothing more than gunpowder. All in all, the Erie Canal was a triumph of determination and sheer hard work.

And it paid off. Barges passed through the canal in great numbers, drawn by teams of horses and mules that walked along towpaths at its sides. Trade in the Great Lakes region increased dramatically as a result of the canal. In the first two years after the canal was opened, the number of cargo boats to use the

Buffalo harbor increased by 150 percent. And a substantial portion of the settlers who made their way into Ohio, Indiana, Illinois, and Michigan did so by way of the Erie Canal. As much as any other event in Monroe's life, the building of the Erie Canal helped promote the westward growth and expansion of the United States in which he believed so strongly.

Monroe was impressed with this swift new method of travel and recommended that the navy acquire some steamships. In recognition of his enthusiasm, one of the first Mississippi River steamboats was named the *James Monroe*. In 1819, it docked at the tiny Louisiana town of Fort Miro; it was the first steamboat to go up the Ouachita River. The people of Fort Miro promptly rechristened their town Monroe, in honor of both the ship and the President.

The Grip of Panic

The year 1819 also brought an economic crisis to the United States. The European price of cotton, America's major export, fell. At the same time, the cost of manufactured goods from the great industrial towns of England rose. Money began to tighten up throughout the United States, and many people who had invested in real estate or shares in trading companies lost their savings. A number of banks went bankrupt; the money they had circulated was suddenly worthless. And it was discovered that the directors of the National Bank were dishonest. This discovery touched off a panic, as citizens tried to turn in their paper money for gold. There was not enough gold to redeem all the paper money, however, and public confidence in the government's economic policies was shaken.

Monroe himself lost money in the Panic of 1819. He knew that he had to restore the people's confidence in the government, so he undertook another goodwill tour, this time through the South, which had been hardest hit by the financial troubles. He asked Congress to raise the tariffs on all imported goods to allow American-made products to compete in the marketplace. He also reduced government spending, limiting such projects as road-building and the construction of more coastal forts.

Gradually, the economy returned to normal. But the concentration of wealth and manufacturing in the Northeast, as opposed to the cash-poor agricultural economy of the South and West, began to drive the regions apart. As the gulf between parts of the country widened and the good feeling of the era began to fade, the stage was set for the final major crisis of Monroe's first term.

SLAVE STATE OR FREE?

During the early years of the 1800s, the western territories were divided into new states. In December of 1817, Mississippi was admitted to the union as the 20th state. It was soon followed by Illinois in 1818 and Alabama in 1819.

This surge of expansion created trouble with the Indians, who were either pushed westward or driven into reservations. During Monroe's time, Indian matters were handled by the Department of War, and the Indians were generally regarded as enemies, with few or no rights. Although little was actually done about the Indian problem during his administration, Monroe was one of the first public officials to sympathize with the plight of the Indians. He felt that it was the government's responsibility to help, not just to exterminate, the native

Americans. A treaty with the Chickasaw nation was signed during his second year in office, and one of his final acts as President would be to set aside a vast tract of land for their use.

But the Indian problem weighed less heavily on Monroe's mind than the growing issue of slavery. Although the European nations were beginning to outlaw the slave trade on moral grounds, slave ownership in the United States was still viewed in practical or political terms, rather than in moral terms.

The slave states of the South had no intention of abandoning the practice of slaveholding; they believed it was vital to their agricultural economy. The free states of the North, whose economy was based on manufacturing and trade, had no need of slaves. But the states of the South tended to support each other against legislation favored by the North, and vice versa. Each side feared that the other would gain greater political power. The South, especially, feared that the North would outstrip it in growth and influence. As a result, each time a new state was created, the question of slavery had to be considered.

In 1819, the two sides seemed equal. Of the 22 states, 11 were slave states and 11 were free. Then Missouri applied to be admitted to the union. Immediately the question arose: Is Missouri to be a slave state or a free state? Most people in Missouri were slaveholders and assumed that theirs would be a slave state.

The Missouri Compromise

Because the population of the northern states was greater than that of the southern states, the North had more members in the House of Representatives. These members argued that slavery was now recognized as immoral by civilized countries everywhere and should be abolished in all the new lands of the Louisiana Purchase. (Of course, they had another motive—they did not want the slave states to outnumber the free states in Congress.) When the question came before Congress in the session of 1819–1820, some people expected the President to settle the issue of slavery once and for all for the entire country.

Slavery was a complicated emotional issue for Monroe. He was a slaveholder and a Southerner, and he had been brought up to regard slavery as normal (he was kind and generous to his slaves, never cruel). But, like Jefferson and Madison, his fellow Southerners, Monroe was wise enough to see into the future.

England and other countries were making slave trading illegal. Haiti, a slave colony in the Caribbean, had revolted and gained independence. Times were changing. Monroe knew that the days of the great slave plantations were numbered and that slavery was an issue that could tear the United States apart. He also knew that he could not enforce a widespread change, so he encouraged Congress to search for a temporary solution. The result was the Missouri Compromise, worked out by Congress with Monroe's full support.

Under the Missouri Compromise, Missouri was admitted into the union in 1820 as a slave state, but Maine was admitted at the same time as a free state. This kept the number of states on each side even: 12 and 12. The Compromise also settled the problem for the remainder of the Louisiana Purchase lands. Slavery was legal south of a line that ran along the latitude of 36 degrees, 30 minutes. It was forever banned north of that line.

A New Country for American Slaves

Monroe knew that the Missouri Compromise was not a final answer to the problem of slavery in the United States. He also knew that his support of the Compromise had lost him some friends among the extremists on both sides of the issue. But he felt that it was the best he or Congress could do in the interest of bringing new states into the union. And the Compromise did solve the problem for the short term. It helped put off for more than 30 years the crisis that was to pit the South against the North in the Civil War.

In the meantime, Monroe became involved in another short-lived attempt to solve the problem of slavery. Along with Jefferson, Henry Clay, Francis Scott Key, and many other prominent Americans, he supported the American Colonization Society (ACS), a group that had been founded in 1817 to help send freed black slaves to new homes in Africa. Many people have criticized the ACS plan, both at the time and ever since, saying that a proposal to send blacks "back to Africa" was a hypocritical attempt to hide the problem instead of allowing blacks to become integrated into American society. The ACS proposal was indeed unrealistic: there were far too many blacks in America to be shipped back to Africa. Moreover, many of them wanted to remain in the United States.

Nevertheless, the ACS did succeed in setting up an African colony for freed, educated black Americans in 1820. That colony became the independent black republic of Liberia in 1847. Because President Monroe had obtained funds from Congress to help the ACS get the colony started, Liberia's capital city was named Monrovia.

Chapter 6

The Monroe Doctrine

The year 1820 was a satisfying one for President Monroe. The nation was beginning to recover from the financial panic of the year before. The Missouri Compromise had solved the tormenting issue of slavery, if only temporarily. The acquisition of Florida was under way. In March, Maria Hester, the Monroes' younger daughter, was married to Samuel Gouverneur; she was the first President's daughter to have a White House wedding. And, as the year went on, it became clear that Monroe would be reelected for a second term.

Because the Federalist Party had completely collapsed, there was really only one political party in the United States, the Republicans. Any challenge to Monroe would come from Republicans who disagreed with his policies or wanted to take over leadership of the country. But, although such men as Henry Clay and Andrew Jackson had presidential ambitions, no one had the enormous support necessary to compete with the popular, respected Monroe. As a result, Monroe had no opposition.

At that time, presidential elections were decided by the vote of the electoral college rather than by a nationwide election of individual votes. When the electoral college met on December 5, 1820, Monroe received 231 of 235 possible votes.

Three electors had died and had not been replaced, and one elector—William Plumer, of New Hampshire—cast his vote for John Quincy Adams, even though he knew that Monroe would win. Plumer reportedly voted for Adams because he believed that no President other than George Washington should receive the honor of being elected unanimously.

Monroe's second term began in March of 1821, when he was sworn in by his old comrade John Marshall, now chief justice of the Supreme Court. Marshall had served with Monroe on Governor Jefferson's Executive Council in 1782. Now, almost 40 years later, the two men who had once played cards and sampled the pleasures of theaters and taverns together had risen to two of the highest offices in the land. The Marine Corps band played at Monroe's inauguration, starting a tradition that continues to this day.

THE OLD WORLD AND THE NEW

Much of Monroe's attention during his second term was directed toward international diplomacy. Midway through the term, he made a statement of United States policy that received little attention at the time. Nevertheless, this policy helped establish the United States as one of the leading powers in the world. It guided America's relations with foreign nations for more than a century after Monroe's death. It is called the Monroe Doctrine, in honor of the President who first put it into words, and it got its start in far-away South America.

Central and South America seemed very remote and unimportant to most Americans in the early 19th century. The southern lands had been claimed by Spain centuries ago, and they remained Spanish colonies. They had little contact with North America; most of their trade was with the parent country, Spain. But the attitude of these colonies toward Spain grew increasingly hostile as their resources—silver, tin, sugar, and lumber—went to enrich wealthy Spanish investors. Inspired by the American and French revolutions, many people in Latin America began to speak of freedom and independence.

Around 1806, a series of liberators rose up in the Spanish New World colonies. The best-known and most successful of these were Francisco de Miranda, Simón Bolívar, and José de San Martín. They raised armies and marched against the Spanish, proclaiming independent new republics in the lands that are now Venezuela, Colombia, Ecuador, Bolivia, Peru, Chile, and Argentina. At the same time, Brazil declared itself independent of its parent country, Portugal. By 1820, the liberation of most of the South American continent was complete. Spain, weakened by an invasion from France and a revolution at home, had been unable to hold onto its colonies. Monroe and others now began to ponder two important questions: How should we treat these newborn republics? And will Spain and the other European powers try to get them back?

A Call For Recognition

From the beginning, the leaders of the new South American nations asked for recognition from the United States. Recognition was and is an important political step. For one country to recognize another means that the first country considers the second one to be a stable, legitimate part of the world community. Recognition is usually followed by the exchange of diplomats and often by trade or defense treaties.

Many people in the United States believed that the country should extend immediate recognition to Colombia, Bolivia, and the other new South American nations. After all, they reasoned, these young republics had much in common with the United States. They, too, had revolted against political and economic oppression and sent their oppressors packing back to the Old World.

It was then a widely held belief in the United States that

the Old World and the New World were completely different in their political philosophies. The Old World (Europe, including Russia) was caught up in a centuries-old tradition of maintaining rule by royalty. The New World, settled by pioneers and free spirits, was designed to house independent states ruled by the people. Many believed that the two hemispheres should have as little to do with one another as possible. George Washington, in his farewell address to the nation, had expressed this view; Jefferson had repeated it in his first inaugural address. It helped shape Monroe's thoughts and eventually appeared in the Monroe Doctrine.

A Cautious Hesitation

But Monroe was cautious about recognizing the new Latin American states. The negotiations with Spain over Florida had dragged on from 1819 until 1821. Not wishing to upset Spain by recognizing the independence of its former colonies, Monroe waited until the ink was dry on the Florida treaty before he considered the question. He also wondered whether Colombia, Venezuela, and the other new countries would remain stable. Perhaps further revolutions and divisions were in store. Soon after the onset of the South American liberation movement, Bolívar and San Martín had quarreled, several of the new republics had fallen apart and been reformed, and others were already at war with one another. Monroe therefore sent three commissioners on a navy boat to visit the capitals of the new republics and advise him about their stability. Their reports were not very encouraging; this provided yet another reason why Monroe moved slowly in offering diplomatic recognition.

Monroe didn't oppose independence for South America. But he did fear that premature alliances with the former European colonies could be disastrous for the United States if Spain or her European allies tried to regain control in South

America. Spain was now controlled by France, and France was allied with the so-called Holy Alliance of Russia, Austria, and Prussia (Germany). These European powers might do more than just resent America's support of the rebel nations — they might actually move against the United States itself. A decade after the War of 1812, this was a prospect that no one in the United States wanted.

Thus, Monroe hesitated. By 1822, however, it was clear that the independence of Mexico and the South American colonies was established. The Spanish had evacuated their last stronghold, in Lima, Peru. Monroe decided to end the wait; these new republics had earned recognition. Congress voted the President the sum of $100,000 to pay for ministers to the new nations. By May, Manuel Torres of Colombia was established in Washington as the first official representative of a South American country.

The Old World Returns

But the threat of European intervention seemed to grow stronger in 1823. France sent troops to subdue a revolutionary movement in Spain, and rumors spread that France and the Holy Alliance were planning to move against the revolutionary governments in South America as well. Also, the United States was forced to consider two other issues that related to political differences between the Old World and the New.

One of these issues was Russia's encroachment in the American Northwest. At that time, Russia owned the Alaska Territory. Tsar Alexander I of Russia announced that no foreign ships could enter the waters for 100 miles off the shore of Russian territory—a move that hurt U.S. shipping and trade. In the meantime, Russian traders and settlers had been moving south, down the Pacific coast. By 1823, they had set up a trading post at Fort Ross, not far from San Francisco. Monroe knew that he had to stop this Russian advance.

The other issue concerned Greece. For years, Greece had been part of the Ottoman (Turkish) Empire. But a revolutionary government had just seized the country and proclaimed its independence from the Ottomans. No European country had yet extended diplomatic recognition to the new Greek government, but many Americans wanted to do so because they felt that the United States should support the cause of liberty against tyranny everywhere in the world. Again Monroe hesitated. He had feared European interference in American affairs; was it thus proper for the United States to take action in a European matter?

As these issues were brewing, England urged the United States to join with it in a statement of policy on Latin America. In London, British foreign minister George Canning told Richard Rush, the United States minister to England, that the two countries should act together to prevent any aggression by Spain, France, or the Holy Alliance. Canning wanted the two countries to announce that England and the United States would intervene—forcibly, if necessary—if any country other than Spain took action in the Spanish Empire. But England refused to recognize the independence of the new South American republics. This made Rush suspect that perhaps England was hoping to claim some of South America as its own.

Sage Advice From the Secretary of State

At home, Monroe at first felt that there was much to be gained by joining with England in a policy statement. He knew that the British navy was the strongest on earth and that the United States did not have the military strength to act alone against Spain or any other European power. But Secretary of State John Quincy Adams thought otherwise. He felt that the United States should stand alone, even though it could not back up its policy by force of arms. After all, he told Monroe, if Spain or France did indeed send an army into the the Western Hemisphere, America wouldn't have to fight, since England would be certain to do so for her.

In addition, Adams did not want to appear too closely linked with British interests; he had been a Federalist until 1808, when he joined the Republican Party, and the Federalists (including his father, President John Adams) had always favored good relations with England. Adams was ambitious to become President after Monroe, and he feared that a favorable reaction to Canning's proposal would look like the act of an old Federalist rather than a sincere Republican. He knew that he would need the support of many powerful Republicans in order to be elected.

For these reasons, Adams urged Monroe to act independently of England. The President then turned to his friends and predecessors in office, Thomas Jefferson and James Madison, for advice. Both older men felt that the United States should join with England in making the policy statement, but both added that it would be better to do it alone than to do nothing. Europe must be warned not to interfere with affairs in the Americas.

In the end, Adams' advice prevailed. Monroe decided not to tie the United States to England. He knew, however, that he had to take some action. During November of 1823, he met with his Cabinet repeatedly to discuss the United States' stand on two issues: Russia's expansion in the Pacific Northwest and the possible European intervention in Latin America. The result of these long, agitated meetings was a historic message to the world.

HANDS OFF THE WESTERN HEMISPHERE

On December 2, 1823, Monroe made his seventh annual speech to Congress. In that year, his message contained very little about domestic affairs. It was concerned with international politics, and it was aimed at the world, not just at the United States Congress.

In his speech, Monroe laid the foundations of what came to be known as the Monroe Doctrine (a doctrine is a principle or belief). The gist of the Monroe Doctrine is simple: The Eastern and Western hemispheres are two distinct realms, and they may not interfere in one another's affairs. This is the philosophy that was shared by most Americans of the time. They cherished the notion that America (and they were willing to include South America) had a special destiny and was completely separate from the Old World of royalty, inherited wealth and privilege, and attendant oppression.

The Four Principles

The Monroe Doctrine had four distinct parts:

(1) Western nations were fundamentally different from European nations; they were republics rather than monarchies.
(2) "The American continents, by the free and independent condition which they have assumed and maintain, are henceforth not to be considered as subjects for future colonization by European powers." In other words, the Americas were closed to new colonization, although the United States would not object to or interfere with existing colonies, such as those in the Caribbean.
(3) Any attempt by any European nation to force its political system on a nation in the Western Hemisphere would be regarded by the United States as a hostile act. This meant that the United States was setting itself up as the protector of the entire hemisphere.
(4) Because Europe and the Americas were now to be regarded as separate, the United States would not interfere in the internal affairs or wars of the European powers.

With plenty of help from Secretary of State John Quincy Adams, Monroe drafted the speech that contained the Monroe Doctrine while sitting at this desk. The desk was made during the reign of King Louis XVI of France, who lost his throne in the French Revolution. (James Monroe Museum and Memorial Library.)

In short, Monroe's message to the world that December was: "You leave America alone, and it will leave you alone." It was a bold statement—even a high-handed one—from a nation that was recovering from bankruptcy and had almost been wiped out in a war with England a decade earlier. But it did have the effect of halting Russian encroachment on the Pacific frontier. And, as a result of the fourth principle, it delayed American recognition of Greece's new government until after some European nations had recognized it.

The Monroe Doctrine was not new or revolutionary. It did not put forth original thinking; instead, it captured the popular opinion of the time. It reflected the concerns of men such as Jefferson, Henry Clay, and John Quincy Adams as well as Monroe. In fact, historians today agree that the principles Monroe put before the world in his 1823 speech were largely worked out by Adams. But it was Monroe who made the decision to put these principles together into a single statement of American policy and to make that statement publicly, refusing a partnership with England. For this reason, the Monroe Doctrine deserves to be named after the President who brought it into being.

THE MONROE DOCTRINE AT WORK

The Monroe Doctrine had little effect on the world for some time after it was issued. Congress did not vote on it, as they would a treaty. Most Americans regarded Monroe's speech as a specific response to the problems of Russia, Greece, and South America, rather than as a policy to guide future actions. In fact, Monroe's speech was not recognized as a formal doctrine for some years. American statesmen referred to it as "Mr. Monroe's message" until the 1850s, when the term "Monroe Doctrine" came into use.

Some statesmen and newspaper editorialists in Europe

reacted with indignation to Monroe's message; some ignored it altogether. Even the United States government did not always bear it in mind. On four occasions during the 1820s, South American leaders tried to form alliances with the United States along the lines laid out in the message. But the United States was not interested in alliances that might someday put it at war with more powerful nations. The British occupied the Falkland Islands in 1833 and the French blockaded Mexico and Argentina in 1838, and the United States took no action against either nation.

But in 1845, President James Polk referred to Monroe's message in a matter concerning territory in Oregon that was claimed by both the United States and England. He also warned European nations not to interfere in the war between Mexico and the United States in 1846. And in the 1860s, the Monroe Doctrine was cited when the United States protested against Spain's attempt to recapture the Dominican Republic and against Napoleon III's attempt to set up an empire in Mexico. After Spain and France backed down from their attempts, most nations admitted that the Monroe Doctrine had become the governing force in American affairs.

Additions to the Doctrine

By 1870, the Monroe Doctrine was felt by all Americans to reflect their nation's strength and importance. Over the next few decades, the Doctrine was interpreted in new ways as new political situations developed. Additions were made to its principles. One such addition was made by President Ulysses S. Grant. Called the "no-transfer" principle, it stated that existing colonies or territories in the New World could not be swapped or sold among European nations. Later, in connection with the development of the Panama Canal, Presidents Rutherford B. Hayes and Theodore Roosevelt said to the world that a canal across Central America was of no concern to Europe, and that European nations had better not try to interfere.

In 1895, President Grover Cleveland used the Doctrine to stand up to England. When England's South American colony of Guiana entered into a border dispute with the independent country of Venezuela, Cleveland insisted that England could not settle the matter alone but must allow the United States to arbitrate it. Although not pleased, England gave in.

The last addition to the Monroe Doctrine was made by Theodore Roosevelt in 1904–1905. Called the Roosevelt Corollary, it states that, if a nation in the Western Hemisphere defaulted on a debt or mistreated foreign subjects, the United States had the right to take action against that nation, thus preventing a European nation from doing so. Thus, the Roosevelt Corollary set up the United States as the international police force of the entire hemisphere. In 1939, President Franklin D. Roosevelt cancelled the Roosevelt Corollary as part of his "Good Neighbor Policy" toward Latin America.

By 1939, in fact, the Monroe Doctrine was becoming a thing of the past. The danger of European colonial ventures in the New World had passed its peak after France's failure in Mexico in the 1860s. The nations of Europe had turned their attention to carving up Africa and the Far East; they left the Americas alone during the second half of the 19th century. At the same time, the United States was growing in wealth and influence. By the time of World War I, no nation could pretend that America was anything but a world power. The two hemispheres could no longer exist as separate realms of influence—the world had grown too small.

In addition, many Central Americans and South Americans had grown resentful of the Monroe Doctrine because it placed them not only under the protection but also under the scrutiny and supervision of the United States. While it was true that the United States was the richest and most powerful nation in the Western Hemisphere, other nations chafed at having America automatically assume the position of leader. As the nations to the south gained stronger political and cultural identities, they found references to the Monroe Doctrine increasingly offensive. Finally, in Buenos Aires in 1936, a group of American countries proposed an agreement which would forbid them to intervene in one another's internal or international affairs. The United States signed the agreement, and the Monroe Doctrine thereafter ceased to be an element in U.S. relations with Central and South America.

Although the Monroe Doctrine was occasionally mentioned during the 1930s and after, it had very little substance after World War I. This global conflict proved that the isolation of one nation or one hemisphere was no longer possible. Today, the Monroe Doctrine is of historical rather than political interest. But, although it plays no part in current world affairs, it was a cornerstone of American policy throughout a century of early growth.

Chapter 7

After the White House

The speech containing the Monroe Doctrine is what President James Monroe is best remembered for, but at the time he did not suspect that his message would go down in history bearing his name. After his message to Congress in December of 1823, he calmly prepared to serve out the final year of his second term. There were as yet no rules that stopped a President from serving more than two terms, and Monroe had many supporters who urged him to serve again. But he was 66 years old in 1824, no longer in the best of health, and ready to retire soon to Oak Hill with Elizabeth.

Monroe hoped that he would be remembered for the "era of good feeling" that he had helped to create. He saw with distress, however, that the race to succeed him in the White House was rapidly eroding the good feelings among the nation's Republican leaders. William Crawford had the support of the South, Andrew Jackson that of the West, John Quincy Adams that of New England. Henry Clay also had a following, mostly in Tennessee. Monroe did not campaign on behalf of any of the candidates, but he let it be known that he thought Adams would be a good successor. Although Crawford campaigned vigorously, most people felt that there had been enough southern Presidents for a while and that his chances of success were slim. In the end, it was Adams who was successful. He then made Clay secretary of state.

During his final year in office, Monroe carried out several projects that were dear to his heart. He submitted a recommendation to Congress calling for funds to enlarge and strengthen the army and navy, in order that "Mr. Monroe's message" could be backed by force, if it became necessary. He also proposed that the government set up a special department to act as the guardian of all native Americans; his recommendation was later put into effect as the Bureau of Indian Affairs. While still in office, Monroe arranged for a grant of land west of the Mississippi River to be set aside as Indian territory. In December of 1824, in his final annual message to Congress, he urged that more such grants be made in the years ahead. Monroe was one of the first American statesmen to recognize that the white settlers and government had a responsibility to the tribes whose land they were so eager to take over.

A FRIEND FROM THE PAST

The year 1824 was a special one both for Monroe and for the entire United States. One of the greatest revolutionary war heroes, the Marquis de Lafayette, was touring the country with his son, George Washington Lafayette. After 40 years, the Marquis had expressed a desire to see America again, but he was too poor to pay for the trip. Monroe asked Congress to help Lafayette, pointing out that he had done more than any other foreigner in the cause of American liberty. Congress generously voted Lafayette $200,000 and a township in Florida.

Lafayette's ship docked in New York Harbor. The Marquis asked one of the officers to recommend a hotel; he had no idea that he was to be an honored guest throughout his entire visit. He was welcomed at the home of Vice-President

Tompkins in New York, then toured New England, where every community staged parades and festivities in his honor. Then he was brought to Washington to be greeted by Monroe.

Standing side by side, Monroe and Lafayette represented two of the last living symbols of the glorious days of the American Revolution. No doubt they realized this—they may have reminisced about the time Monroe had helped the wounded Marquis from the field during the Battle of Brandywine, back in 1777. Congress then ushered in 1825 with a New Year's Day dinner in honor of the Marquis de Lafayette, a hero of the Revolution, and James Monroe, the last Revolutionary President.

POVERTY AND GRIEF

In March of 1825, the Monroes left Washington for Oak Hill. By this time the house was surrounded by a grove of handsome poplars that swayed in the breeze blowing from the top of nearby Sugar Loaf Mountain. Monroe loved these poplars, for he had planted them himself—one for every state in the union.

Unfortunately, he was not to enjoy the long, happy retirement he had dreamed of. The money problems that had plagued him on and off during his entire political career were now worse than ever. He had spent money from his own pocket in government service for years—ever since his first mission to France in 1794—and he had never been reimbursed for any of it. In 1824, shortly before leaving office, he submitted many years' worth of claims and accounts to Congress. He hoped that he would receive some sort of grant, like the one that had been given to Lafayette; at the very least, he expected to have his old accounts settled.

But Congress delayed and delayed. Monroe had no savings and, at 67 years of age, after many years of full-time public service, no profession. To make matters worse, he owed money to people who had ignored his debts while he was President but now demanded payment; John Jacob Astor was one such creditor. Monroe began selling his property to raise money to live on: first the estate at Highland, then land he owned in Virginia and Kentucky.

Thomas Jefferson would have gladly helped Monroe—except for the fact that he, too, had been bankrupted by public service. In the year of Jefferson's death, a national fund-raising drive was finally set in motion to help the former President. Monroe was not so lucky. He continued to sell his land, and in 1826 he began to sell his slaves.

Lafayette, who had benefitted from the generosity of Congress at President Monroe's urging, wrote to Monroe in 1828 with an offer of money. But Monroe felt too great a sense of pride and dignity to take anything from a man to whom America owed so much. He continued to ask Congress to review his claim, but nothing happened, even though the citizens of Virginia and New York sent petitions to Washington on Monroe's behalf.

Troubles to the End

Elizabeth Monroe had been unwell for many years with several chronic illnesses, and now Monroe's health began to suffer as well. He fell from his horse in 1828, receiving a severe concussion that was followed by a fever. He managed to recover, but this mishap was immediately followed by several more grievous difficulties.

First came a bitter controversy with Andrew Jackson that exhausted much of the former President's strength. Jackson planned to run for President and wanted to clear up the old matter of his Florida adventure in 1818. He and his friends began a campaign in the press to persuade the public that Jackson had had a secret deal with President Monroe authorizing him to capture Florida by force. The business of John

Rhea, the mysterious messenger, was dragged up again, and Monroe was forced to refute Jackson's allegations.

Worse troubles were in store. After 44 years of marriage, his wife Elizabeth died in 1830. Monroe was so consumed with grief that he wanted to delay the burial as long as possible. Soon after this tragedy, Monroe's son-in-law, George Hay, died.

Oak Hill had become not only expensive, but lonely and filled with sad memories. Monroe moved to his daughter Maria Gouverneur's house in New York City, although it is not clear whether he merely planned a long visit or intended to take up permanent residence there. Early in 1831, he put Oak Hill up for sale.

Monroe's time in New York was quiet, sometimes somber. He worked on an autobiography and corresponded with James Madison, one of his few surviving friends. John Quincy Adams visited Monroe several times when business took him to New York. Aside from that, Monroe's only recreation seems to have been taking walks along the docks of New York Harbor. Clad still in his velvet knee-breeches and buckled shoes, Monroe by this time looked like an echo of a bygone era, a living picture from a history book.

By late spring of 1831, Monroe's health was failing fast. He was bedridden in Maria's home and calmly waiting to die. But Andrew Jackson did not want Monroe to slip away without clearing his name. He produced a man named John Rhea, from Tennessee, who claimed that Monroe had indeed given him secret orders to be delivered to Jackson in Florida. From the depths of his illness, the tired old President issued a public statement in a trembling voice, denying that he had ever seen Rhea or given him a message. The public grew indignant at this badgering, and it was generally considered that Jackson had gone too far. Like Hamilton years before in the Reynolds blackmail scandal, Jackson let the matter drop.

By then, it hardly mattered to Monroe. Even his long financial struggle was eased a bit. Congress awarded him a grant of $30,000. It was only half of his claim, and it was barely enough to pay his debts, but he was glad to have the business settled. Soon after, on the afternoon of Independence Day, July 4, 1831, Monroe died. He was 73 years old.

The End of an Era

Monroe's final years had been spent in poverty and obscurity, but he received a hero's burial. His hearse, draped with black and gold cloths, was driven up New York City's Broadway to the cemetery, and thousands of mourners followed in a quiet procession. The guns of the Battery—one of the fortifications Monroe had inspected on his triumphal tour in 1817—fired a 73-gun salute, one gun each minute for more than an hour. Around the country, church bells tolled, army and navy cannon fired salutes, and people wore black armbands in mourning.

Monroe's death represented more than the passing of a former President and an honored public servant. It was the end of an era. One of America's last living links with its heritage had died. Monroe was the last President to have lived through the stirring events of the nation's birth. As a young man, he had rubbed elbows with George Washington, Ben Franklin, and other Founding Fathers. He was a hero of the American Revolution who had nearly lost his life in defense of freedom. He had brought the country through the terrible War of 1812. And, as one who believed in the greatness of the United States, he had done his best throughout his lifetime to support and increase that greatness. Monroe's great contribution was that he made the United States see itself not as a collection of states or regions but as a unified nation, with a common purpose at home and an important place in the world.

In 1858, 100 years after Monroe's birth, his remains were transferred from New York City to this tomb in Hollywood Cemetery, Richmond, Virginia. (U.S. Army Photograph.)

Monroe's remains lay in the Gouverneur vault in New York for many years. Then, in 1858, on the 100th anniversary of his birth, the people of Virginia voted the funds to transfer the remains to his home state. Monroe was reburied with great ceremony in Richmond. The last of the Virginia Presidents was home in Virginia at last.

Bibliography

Ammon, Harry. *James Monroe: The Quest for National Identity.* New York: McGraw-Hill, 1951. This book focuses on Monroe's activities as diplomat and President, and on his role in defining the young United States through the Louisiana Purchase and the Monroe Doctrine.

Cresson, W.P. *James Monroe.* Chapel Hill: University of North Carolina Press, 1946. Although it is a little dry, this is a detailed examination of Monroe's entire life.

Donovan, Frank. *Mr. Monroe's Message: The Story of the Monroe Doctrine.* New York: Dodd, Mead, 1963. In simple terms, this book summarizes the background and effects of the Monroe Doctrine.

Gerson, Noel B. *James Monroe: Hero of American Diplomacy.* Englewood Cliffs, New Jersey: Prentice-Hall, 1969. This short biography of Monroe was written especially for young readers. Though it skips some interesting details of his life and times, it is lively and colorful.

Hanser, Richard. *The Glorious Hour of Lieutenant Monroe.* New York: Atheneum, 1976. Monroe's exciting experiences during the War of Independence are the subject of this book, which offers a good background to the conflict and vivid descriptions of battles.

Hoyt, Edwin P. *James Monroe.* Chicago: Reilly & Lee, 1968. This is a well-balanced, simple, and brief look at Monroe's life and achievements.

Levine, Isaac Don. *Hands Off the Panama Canal.* Washington, D.C.: Monticello Press, 1976. This short book explains how the Monroe Doctrine applies to Central America.

May, Ernest R. *The Making of the Monroe Doctrine.* Cambridge, Massachusetts: Harvard University Press, 1975. May explores the political and philosophical background of the speech that is now called the Monroe Doctrine. He also explains John Quincy Adams' part in forming the Doctrine.

Monroe, James. *Autobiography.* Edited by Stuart Gerry Brown. Syracuse, New York: Syracuse University Press, 1959. Monroe's own account of his life emphasizes his diplomatic missions and his years in the White House, downplaying his early life, personal feelings, and experiences. Nevertheless, it is interesting because it explains his beliefs about the importance of the West and the Monroe Doctrine.

Styron, Arthur. *The Last of the Cocked Hats: James Monroe and the Virginia Dynasty.* Norman, Oklahoma: University of Oklahoma Press, 1945. This book looks at Monroe's place in the string of southern statesmen that included Washington, Jefferson, and Madison. It gives a good account of Monroe's personal and political relationships with these men.

Wilmerding, Lucius. *James Monroe: Public Claimant.* New Brunswick, New Jersey: Rutgers University Press, 1960. The subject of this book is Monroe's financial difficulties and his efforts to get money from the government near the end of his life.

Index